The Crown of England

St. Edward's Crown. Used for the act of Coronation. Richly adorned with diamonds,
emeralds, sapphires, rubies and pearls. This heavy crown is exchanged for a lighter one—
the Imperial Crown—before the King leaves Westminster Abbey.

CORONATION
SOUVENIR BOOK
1937

by

Gordon Beckles

Art Editor : Ivor Castle

A DAILY EXPRESS PUBLICATION, LONDON, 1937

HIS book tells by word and picture the story of two Royal brothers ; of one whose brief reign ended so unfortunately last year ; and of the other who has now been crowned as King in his place.

As time tempers the memory of Edward the Eighth's ten months' reign, there seems less and less reason that such memory be a tragic one. Edward had served his Empire through twenty-five of its most tempestuous years. His task during two decades was no less arduous than that performed by his august father King George the Fifth : nor less important in re-binding the war-frayed tissues of Empire.

Twenty-five years of such service—with scant shelter from the scorching glare of public adulation and curiosity—is a career in itself for any man.

So Edward made it : a career.

Not as Edward the Eighth but as Prince of Wales will he remain in the memories of his subjects.

Edward's brother—blessed with wife and children—is now our King ; nor did his Coronation come before the nation had time to discover in him unsuspected strains of that strange charm which had always been one of Edward's assets. Of the sterner virtues possessed by King George the Sixth no one has ever had any doubt ; they are the virtues of authentic kingship.

This volume tries to portray the pageant of fifteen stirring months as objectively as possible, neither with prejudice nor sentiment, but as they unfolded themselves to the world at the time.

Gordon Beckles.

KING GEORGE V

KING EDWARD VIII

KING GEORGE VI

King Edward's Brief Reign Begins

The Accession. Oath of Allegiance is taken in Parliament and the new King proclaimed "Our only lawful and rightful Liege Lord Edward the Eighth."

CHAPTER ONE

THE sun set in a scarlet glow on January 20th, 1936, and the flat fen country stretching to the west of Sandringham's wooded plateau was bathed in the rich light.

Propped up in a chair facing the sunset sat King George the Fifth—in Sandringham House—moving uneasily between the worlds of dream and reality.

In the next room sat the Prince of Wales, flown back from London at noon that day. Darkness fell. The rambling mansion was hushed. The evening moved on and the dying monarch's eyes opened fitfully. At five minutes to one in the morning by the clocks in the house, King George the Fifth peacefully entered upon a glory greater than his own. The Prince by his bedside became King Edward the Eighth. Thus dawned the first of a reign of three hundred and twenty-six days.

The Prince who was now king glanced at his wrist watch. It

3

was set by the time of the outside world, an hour behind the Sandringham time enforced by Edward the Seventh. The man who had just been addressed as "Your Majesty" by the Archbishop of Canterbury gave his first command as King.

"Put the clocks back to the proper time," he said.

That was not the disregard of sentiment that some thought ; it was a practical gesture ; the Norfolk mansion was now the centre of the British Empire and endless confusion would ensue if arrangements were not synchronised.

His Modern Ideas

The new King was a practical man. Those of us who were at Sandringham House that night wondered with the rest of the world what manner of sovereign he would make. He shared few tastes with the monarch now lying dead on the first floor.

He was wholly a young man of his period ; he liked flying, not yachting ; he liked golf, not pheasant shooting ; he enjoyed jazz, not Gounod or Puccini ; he preferred racing cars to ponderous limousines ; the dinner jacket and lounge suit suited him more than evening dress and frock coat.

He was self-willed and fearless, highly-strung but with an authentic vein of the family seriousness in his nature to counteract the boyish high spirits which he was carrying with him into middle age ; a young man who deplored pomposity and who would much rather chat with an artisan than an ambassador.

MOURNING SONS
King Edward and brothers in funeral procession at Sandringham.

For all the publicity showered on him for over a quarter of a century Edward Albert Christian George Andrew Patrick David was still a rather enigmatic figure when he came to the throne at the age of forty-one.

And there descended instantly upon him the heavy cloak of kingship through which few monarchs can be seen as they once were before they ascended to a throne.

Thirty-three minutes after his father's death, he used his signature as King for the first time, sending a telegram to the Lord Mayor of London, Sir Percy Vincent :

"I am deeply grieved to inform you that my beloved father, the King, passed away peacefully at 11.55 to-night.
EDWARD

Next morning he started to make history again by being the first British King to fly.

With the Duke of York, his brother, the King flew from Bircham Newton to London to attend the special meeting of the Privy Council summoned to proclaim his accession to the Throne.

The New King's Declaration

It was at this meeting that King Edward made his first declaration to the Nation.

"I am determined," he said, *"to follow in my father's footsteps, and to work, as he did throughout his life, for the happiness and welfare of all classes of my subjects."*

TELLING THE CITY
Proclamation of King Edward, Royal Exchange, January 22, 1936.

Later that same day both Houses of Parliament met to take the Oath of Allegiance. Amid an impressive silence peers, ministers, and members of Parliament took the Oath : "I swear by Almighty God that I will be faithful and bear true allegiance to His Majesty, King Edward, his heirs and successors, according to Law. So help me God."

Public Proclamation

The following morning the Garter Principal King of Arms read the Proclamation from a scarlet draped balcony in Friary Court, St. James's Palace. At the first stroke of ten, golden sleeved trumpeters gave a double fanfare on their instruments. Then the first gun in St. James's Park boomed out while the Garter King of Arms, raising his voice to be heard above the noise of the gunfire, read from a large parchment : that Prince Edward is "with one voice and consent of tongue and heart" proclaimed "our only lawful and rightful Liege Lord Edward the Eighth."

The scene was one of impressive pageantry.

Who dared dream that, before the year was out, these ceremonies would have to be re-enacted ?

The First Ordeal as King

On the solemn sadness of the rest of that first week of the young King's reign there is no need to dwell in this volume. Except, perhaps, to recall the look of gravity and exhaustion on the face of Edward as he trudged along in the biting January wind behind the coffin of his father at Sandringham ; and later that day made the three-mile march from King's Cross to Westminster Hall through darkening streets ; yes, and perhaps to remember the midnight vigil with his three brothers at the Royal bier ; and later on again the memory of that fair-headed, lonely figure in the last procession of all—not riding as kings had ridden through London at his grandfather's funeral—but on foot.

Here, said the nation, was a man capable of seeing things clearly and having them done as he thought they should be done.

WELSH GUARDS "COME OF AGE"
King Edward at London celebration,
All Hallows, St. David's Day, 1936.

CHAPTER TWO

The King inspects work in the liner Queen Mary—and "sees for himself" one of Glasgow's worst slum districts. The Royal "We" and the King's English.

IN March he went to Scotland to see the liner *Queen Mary* at whose christening ceremony by his mother and father he had been present eighteen months before.

He "wanted to see for himself" and he caught the ordinary night express, motored to John Brown's shipyard at Clydebank and set off at his old Prince-of-Wales-pace round the huge liner, then in an advanced stage of construction. He displayed all the curiosity which he and his brother the Duke of York had inherited—together with an uncanny memory for faces—from both his parents : "Who ? Where ? What ? Which ? Why ?"

But the inspection of the *Queen Mary* was but a cloak for a more serious purpose.

On the way back from Clydebank to Glasgow the King diverted his car and visited the Glasgow Corporation housing estate at Knightswood. Although it rained persistently all the time, large crowds stood in the down-pour and cheered lustily. He visited two houses on the estate, in both of which he made inquiries about the rent paid by the occupiers. From Knightswood he decided to go to the Anderston district, one of the worst slums in Glasgow, and went into every home in a tenement in 29 North Street.

At the first door he paused and said, "May I come in ?"

The occupier, blind for thirty years, answered, "Certainly, come right in. Who are you ?"

"I am your King," was the reply, and the King grasped the man's hand in a firm handshake. Perhaps the most delightful encounter of the day was that between a five-year-old boy and the King on the stairs of the Crieff Court tenement.

Seeing the King, the boy boldly asked, "Are yew the noo King ?"

"Yes, sonny," replied King Edward gravely, "I am."

At the City Chambers, where he talked to the Lord Provost, Mr. John Stewart, about his experiences, the King remarked, "The conditions in some of the places I have seen are appalling, but I have seen worse in other places, Durham among them."

Yes, here was a man not afraid to go where his Ministers dare not. Who was determined to carry to the Throne the tradition he had established as Prince of Wales. No reporter present will ever forget the look of pain and surprise on the face of the Prince when he spent those days with the unemployed Durham miners in 1929.

The new King was breaking with tradition as violently as his grandfather had broken with the Victorian tradition thirty-six years before. The Royal "we" became "I," and even the King's English took a distinctive turn of pronunciation—as the world was soon to learn when he made his first broadcast.

It was the English of a man who had travelled. The word "broadcast" was pronounced with the last syllable long in the American manner (he later used the word "progress" with the first syllable accented to rhyme with "frog"), and there was even a hint of Cockney—or was it huntin' English?—in the pronunciation of some words.

Certainly no part of an Empire which speaks a thousand and one variations of English could complain that the King's was an Oxford English.

No, here was a man. One whose motto was as much "Let's Get On With It" as "Ich Dien"—one who could be sure that tens of millions of voices would be raised in acclamation when he said "I AM YOUR KING !"

CHAPTER THREE

Trouble in Spain ends prospect of Riviera holiday. The King, at Vimy, unveils Memorial to Canada's 60,000 dead. Garden Party surprise for Pilgrims and an ovation in the rain.

NO incident in the reign of Edward VIII was more illuminating than the sequel to the ceremony of the Vimy Ridge memorial to the Canadian dead. It started with the arrival in France of 6,000 Canadian ex-soldiers, who had come

CLYDESIDE CHEERS

VISITING THE LINER QUEEN MARY
King Edward surrounded by Clydebank workmen, March, 1936.

6

MAUNDY MONEY GIFTS
King Edward at the Abbey, with the Archbishop of
Canterbury (right), for centuries-old ceremony.

back at their own expense to pay tribute to 60,000 comrades in arms who gave up their lives for King and Empire in the last war.

They landed at Havre and Antwerp, after a stormy passage, much of it spent in confined quarters and with considerable discomfort. It was a legion of weary, khaki-bereted men of middle age that arrived with three thousand-odd tired women folk at Arras on the day of the unveiling.

FIRST STATE DRIVE AS MONARCH
King Edward leaving Buckingham Palace for a levée at St. James's.

The King's Dilemma

The King was to unveil the Memorial to the men who had captured the strategic ridge in that dawn of twenty years ago and it was going to be the only chance for these men and women from the prairies and pinewoods to see their young King.

But for Edward himself it was a difficult moment. Faced with a year of preparation —and already feeling the strain of the accession ceremonies—he not only needed a rest, looked as if he needed a rest, but *insisted* upon a rest.

Holiday Postponed

The secluded residence of Miss Maxine Elliott—the veteran American actress— had been leased for August and September for the King; it was two miles out of Cannes, with its own beach, but cut off from the main road by the main railway line.

Then trouble broke out in Spain, there was an outpouring of Spanish refugees over the French border which gave the French Government an excellent excuse for advising against a Royal holiday on French territory.

Actually, of course, the whole Riviera was at that time racked by Communistic and other strikes.

When the King arrived at Vimy on the Sunday morning of July 26th, he already knew that he had been robbed of his much-needed holiday in the sun. It was a doubly important occasion, for it was his first visit to foreign soil since his accession and he was being met by President Lebrun.

At Vimy Ridge

He strode down into the arena at the base of the Memorial where stood the ranks of men who had—by crossing the Atlantic at their own cost—recaptured some of the epic feeling of the Canadian contingent which crowded to the help of the Motherland in 1914.

To crimson-coated Corporal Warrior of the Royal Canadian Mounted Police he said : "I'm your commandant. Do you know my ranch ?"

"I do, sir. When are you coming back there ?"

"Ah," said the King, "if only I knew . . ."

When they tried to lead him through the ranks along some sort of pre-arranged route, the King strode the other way.

There he was, smiling and talking to the people in the enclosure, a slim, fair-haired young man in a grey morning coat. You could not resist the contrast with his rather harassed look during the ornate ceremonies on Sunday, nor, indeed, with his last appearance in this very enclosure during the debutantes' garden party.

Out of the Heavens—

But ten minutes later tragedy descended on the garden party. A black rain cloud came driving from the westward and burst with violence over the centre of London. Thousands rushed for shelter in the long refreshment tents ; but hundreds remained in the rain around the enclosure to watch the King—still smiling—ask someone for a cigarette, light it himself and then look with a wry face at the sky.

Ten minutes later, realising that the garden party was going to be swept away anyway, he started to stroll back to the Palace two hundred yards away. Immediately thousands of Canadians sprang from their tea-time dug-outs, dashing across the lawns towards the hatless figure strolling along with a cigarette in his mouth.

Popularity

Two equerries carried umbrellas over his head, but he waved them away. On the top steps leading to the Palace he faced the crowd which a few determined ex-officers had vainly been trying to keep under control and to protect their sovereign from hearty slaps on the back, close-up snaps and even kisses from women.

Then he went into the Palace and a few minutes afterwards came out on the balcony above and held up his hand for silence.

FIRST BRITISH KING TO FLY
King Edward landing at Windsor from Marseilles.

The old want-to-see-for-myself spirit asserted itself, and he chatted with people in the back rows, women who had *not* six sons and men who had merely fought and escaped the good fortune of winning any kind of medal.

They cheered him at the end of the complicated Anglo-French ceremony and he flew back to England.

The Canadians in England.

Now for the sequel ; it took place three days later when the Canadian pilgrims were invited by the Duke and Duchess of Gloucester to a garden party in the grounds of Buckingham Palace.

The day was sunny and the Canadians—in their berets, and some even with their ruck-sacks—spread themselves across the lawns which only one Londoner in a hundred thousand ever treads. Not very exciting ? No, but a pleasant occasion, for most of them had entered through the Mall courtyard, and had a glimpse of the ground floor rooms of the Palace, which had been thrown open.

A quiver went through the little groups. Something was happening in the Royal enclosure just where the band was playing.

The King !

WALKING IN THE RAIN
Informal King Edward on way to Duchy of Cornwall Council Meeting.

ARDENT GOLFER
King Edward (as Prince of Wales) in Parliamentary Golf Handicap.

He spoke in a conversational tone, yet so clearly that those on the outskirts of the crowd a hundred yards away could hear quite clearly.

"None of us who were present at Vimy Ridge on Sunday," he said, one hand in his pocket and the other on the balustrade, "can ever forget that day, and for me, personally, my recollection is vivid because it brought me into contact with Canadians, and whenever I meet Canadians it makes me remember that I have four times been to the Dominion.

"It really was a most moving occasion, tinged, of course, with sadness. To-day we meet under less solemn, certainly happier, but decidedly damper circumstances.

"You know," he went on, "I don't take any responsibility for the weather. I can only hope that you are not getting *too* wet. When I think of how badly needed rain is in some of the Western provinces I can only say that we seem to have got the rain in the wrong place to-day."

He waved his hand at that, and the crowd burst spontaneously—and rather surprisingly—into "Auld Lang Syne." Then they swung into "For He's A Jolly Good Fellow" and finally into "God Save The King."

With Boy Scouts at Windsor

Close on 1,000 Scouts attended this Church parade and were addressed by King Edward.

An unusual Royal Speech

It was a remarkable ten minutes. Kings have not been accustomed to addressing crowds on Palace lawns as if they were all boys together, cracking jokes and getting very wet themselves in the process.

Some of the Palace's liveried servants looked with pained surprise at the veterans as they streamed amiably through the gold and crimson apartments of the Palace as they left.

The Canadians thought it grand ; and so it was. Only a man with a sure nerve and knowledge of men could have worded and fitted that impromptu speech so perfectly to his audience.

The Man with the Revolver on Constitution Hill. World rejoices that the King was unharmed. Kings, Presidents, Dictators—even Communists—join in congratulation.

THURSDAY, July 16th, was a memorable day in the life of King Edward. He was the object of a demonstration by an armed man on Constitution Hill and the whole world throbbed with indignation and excitement.

Monsieur Herriot rose in the Chamber of Deputies in Paris and read a telegram of congratulations to the King which all parties—including the Communists—subscribed to with vociferous applause ; kings and presidents and dictators all over the globe vied with each other in their messages of gratitude that no harm had been done.

The occasion of the incident was the presentation in Hyde Park of new Colours to the Brigade of Guards. And it was notable, too, for a finely delivered speech on more formal lines.

The King gave his address from a platform in the centre of the parade ground. Every word was carried clearly by the microphones to the farthest limits of the vast crowd which had congregated for the ceremony.

"*Grenadiers, Coldstreamers, and Scots Guardsmen :*
"*It is with mingled feelings that I address you on this solemn occasion. I am glad, so soon after becoming Colonel-in-Chief of your respective regiments, to entrust new Colours to your charge. But, when I know that it was His late Majesty, my father's wish in the closing months of his reign to give them to you himself, my heart is full of reverent remembrance of the great example which he set us all, and of the gratitude for his constant interest in the Brigade of Guards during the eventful quarter of a century in which he held the position that I do to-day.*

"*Only a few of us on parade this morning have known the awful weight of war, with all its horrors, and yet its comradeship, during the world struggle of 20 years ago. With*

TROOPING THE COLOUR PAGEANTRY
King Edward heading procession of royal dukes and foreign military
attachés on his 42nd birthday.

all my heart I hope, and indeed I pray, that never again will our age and generation be called upon to face such stern and terrible days. Humanity cries out for peace and the assurance of peace, and you will find in peace opportunities of duty and service as noble as any that bygone battlefields can show.

"Keep then the message of these Colours ever before you, and the honour of your regiment and of your country will rest safe and sure in your hands."

leaning forward to get a better view of the procession; the lively air being played by the massed bands; the mounted figure of the King followed by that of Major-general Sergison-Brooke and his Equerry, Sir John Aird; then suddenly a loaded revolver clattering to the road beneath the hooves of the King's horse.

The King drew his horse up and glanced in the direction from which the missile came.

THE FORT
Air picture of King Edward's country home, Fort Belvedere, in lovely woodland setting. Note bathing pool on right.

Massed bands, immediately preceding the King, played the battalions out of the Park, across Hyde Park Corner, and through the Quadriga Arch. And it was just as the King was emerging from the arch that a man, thrusting his way to the front of the crowd, which at this point was only three or four deep, threw a revolver on the ground in the direction of the King.

It all happened so quickly. The expectant cheering crowds

"That gives us exactly ten seconds, I think," he said to his equerry, and then rode on as though nothing had happened. "The King bore himself as becomes a King, true to the ancient definition that 'a King is he who has no fear'," commented the New York Times.

And the world was thrilled as it read the news of the incident—a purposeless exploit by a misguided fanatic—on the front pages of its newspapers.

WITH THE ROYAL AIR FORCE

King Edward, on his R.A.F. inspection tour, by air, mounts
ladder to "see for himself."

THE KING RODE ON . . . . . .

A few seconds earlier a man had thrown a revolver into the roadway. King Edward was
returning to Buckingham Palace from ceremony of presenting Colours in Hyde Park.

After the "Revolver Incident"

King Edward at the head of the Brigade of Guards, turns, unperturbed, to make inquiry after revolver had been thrown in roadway.

———

(*Left*)
Crowd watches the arrested man taken to police van.

———

(*Right*)
McMahon: He was sentenced to twelve months' hard labour for "producing a revolver with intent to alarm the King."

CURTSY TO HER KING

Débutante presented to King Edward at Royal
Garden Party, Buckingham Palace.

CHAPTER FIVE

Unconventional holiday of an unconventional monarch. Visits to Greek King and Premier. A Gallipoli pilgrimage. Kemal Ataturk's welcome. A self-imposed Press censorship.

ON the 30th July, an official announcement was made at Buckingham Palace that Edward would be going on a cruise along the Dalmatian Coast and in the Eastern Mediterranean. The King had chartered Lady Yule's £300,000 luxury yacht, the Nahlin, a vessel of 1,574 tons, and on August 8th he flew to Calais and there joined the Vienna Express. His dozen or so guests included Mr. Duff Cooper, the Secretary of State for War and Lady Diana Cooper, Major Humphrey Butler—who was on the Duke of Kent's staff—and a Mrs. Ernest Simpson, an American woman married to a Canadian, who had been a close friend of the King during the past two years.

No Council of State had been appointed to act in his absence. It was the unconventional holiday of an unconventional monarch. King Edward VII frequently took Continental jaunts to spas and seaside resorts; fortunately for King Edward VII the Europe of his days was not so infested with snooping American news-scavengers, nor had the Press camera yet come into its own.

The Nahlin cruised along the Dalmatian Coast, dropping anchor here and there while the King went ashore and visited the little towns and villages, chatting freely with the local fisher folk from whom he invariably received a warm reception.

At Novigrad the King, dressed in a dark blue sailor suit (which he had purchased in the island of Rab), and a pair of white tennis shoes, asked a local fisherman if he spoke German. The man signified that he didn't, but when the King then inquired if he spoke English, the man surprisingly replied, "Sure, boss, I speak English. I was 20 years in the States."

The King promptly asked the man to come back with him and the fisherman rowed out to the yacht. Shortly afterwards he was landed again, and when asked what had happened he said, "D'at guy in the blue shirt wanted me to go on board, but I dassn't because I knew de English King was dere."

Anchoring off Biograd one afternoon, the King went ashore and came upon a woman picking maize cobs. After watching her for some time, the King asked if he might buy some to take on board with him. The woman, however, pushed a large bunch into his arms and stubbornly refused to accept any money, adding "You are our guest."

The Orb and the Royal Sceptre with The Cross

The golden Orb is held to signify the dominion of the Christian Church over the world. It is surmounted with a magnificent amethyst, cut in facets, on which stands a richly-jewelled cross. Gold centre fillet and arch are studded with clusters of gems and outlined in pearls.

The Sceptre With The Cross is the symbol of kingly power and justice. It is of gold, and embodies a great drop-shaped Star of Africa diamond. Amethyst at top bears a cross patée containing large emerald and encrusted with diamonds.

When the yacht anchored off the old town of Trogir, just north of Split, the King landed and spent some time going through his letters which had been brought by the destroyer Glowworm from Brindisi. Later, still wearing his sailor suit and white tennis shoes, he rowed out himself to the destroyer and, as he neared the warship, he was heard to call out jokingly, "I am now reviewing the Fleet."

At Dubrovnik the King was followed by huge crowds as he walked through the streets. Failing to shake off a horde of delighted followers who were working their cameras in a frenzy of excitement, the King hastily climbed up on to the ancient ramparts and there smilingly turned the tables on the crowd by levelling his camera at them.

A Visit to Greece

The Nahlin arrived off Corfu on the 21st August, and the King landed and went to the Villa Mibelli where he was entertained by King George II of Greece.

From now on the King's holiday became more strenuous and formal, and when he visited Athens—the first reigning British Monarch to do so—he had a two-hour talk with General Metaxas, the Greek Premier, at the British Legation. Time, however, was found to climb the Acropolis.

After leaving Athens, the Nahlin was driven by a strong gale and heavy seas to take refuge in Karystos Bay at the southern end of the island of Euboea. On the following day the yacht, with the King on board, was involved in a collision with one of the supports of an iron-swing bridge in the narrow strait dividing Euboea from the mainland. The strait is only about 40 yards wide at this point (just off Chalkis), and, although the bridge had been opened, such a strong current was running that the bows of the yacht struck the support. The impact was not severe but, in the wash caused by the destroyers Glowworm and Grafton hurrying forward, two rowing boats capsized, and their occupants had to be rescued.

Gallipoli

The King again created a precedent when he set foot on Turkish soil, landing at Gallipoli on September 3rd. He disembarked at the village of Sedd-el-Bahr where, in 1915, the Allied forces had landed at the beginning of the Gallipoli campaign. He visited the principal cemeteries and battle-fields on the south part of the peninsula, and then went to the Lone Pine Cemetery and New Zealand memorial.

During the yacht's subsequent passage through the Bosphorus both banks had been illuminated by searchlights and the city's many mosques and minarets had been floodlit for the benefit of the Royal visitor.

Kemal Ataturk, President of the Turkish Republic, greeted the King on his arrival, and the Turkish Fleet, cruising off Prinkipo Island fired a salute. Despite the King's wish for no formalities or official reception, thousands of British flags flew from houses and public buildings.

Newspapers devoted their front pages to his visit, giving great prominence to His Majesty's gesture in placing flowers on the grave of the Turkish Unknown Soldier.

AS COLONEL-IN-CHIEF,
THE SEAFORTH HIGHLANDERS

The King talked for some time with Kemal Ataturk on board the yacht, and after dining at the British Embassy, witnessed a "Venetian Night" celebration in which warships and private craft took part.

Earlier in the afternoon, he had visited the famous Serail, former palace and harem of the Sultan, had entered the building carrying his camera, but on learning that the taking of pictures had always been strictly forbidden, he strapped it up again.

At the end of the second day he left at 11 p.m. for Vienna in a special train put at his disposal by Kemal. Crowds cheered as the train moved out of the station.

Remembering Canada's 60,000 Dead

...housands saw King Edward unveil ...is magnificent memorial at Vimy.

GREETING A CANADIAN MOTHER

Another Royal Reception

King Boris of Bulgaria met him with his own special train at a point 60 miles from Sofia, and the Royal party proceeded down the line to Caziceva, where waiting cars took them to King Boris's country palace.

After lunch at the palace the King was taken for a lightning tour round Sofia, and King Boris eventually travelled in the train as far as the Jugo-Slav border.

In Vienna (where he stopped several days and consulted an ear specialist), the King met the Austrian Chancellor, Dr. Schuschnigg, and President Miklas, as well as the Hungarian Foreign Minister. He afterwards travelled by train to Zurich where his own airplane had been sent to carry him back to England. Thus ended an historic holiday, undertaken on his own initiative and without the advice of his Ministers.

Mrs Simpson

Most of the pictures taken during the cruise and the subsequent return by land contained the smartly-clad figure of a woman captioned as "Mrs. Simpson." The English papers—only too well aware of the way in which her name was being linked with that of the King —in nearly all cases removed Mrs. Simpson from the pictures they published.

They imposed upon themselves a censorship; yet hundreds of thousands of people all over the Empire were already gossiping about the American friend of the monarch.

CHAPTER SIX

Last month of the Reign. Visit in rough weather to the Home Fleet. The lower deck—hosts of their King.

THE last month of King Edward's reign opened with a tremendous burst of activity.

Yet the King's programme was typical of the strenuous manner in which he had accustomed himself to approach public duty. On November 11th, he attended the Armistice ceremony at the Cenotaph at 10.45 in the morning; at noon he had returned to Buckingham Palace where, after lunch, he had received visitors, among them the Lord Chamberlain, the Earl of Cromer.

CENTRE OF ATTRACTION

King Edward making for shelter, in rain storm, surrounded by cheering Canadian Vimy pilgrims, his guests at Buckingham Palace.

Then at 4 p.m. he had visited Queen Mary at Marlborough House; at 6.30 p.m. he had gone to the Field of Remembrance at Westminster Abbey and, unnoticed by the other mourners, had planted a wooden cross bearing the inscription "In memory of His Majesty King George V," afterwards trudging hatless in the pouring rain along the pathways by the field; and, finally, he had attended the British Legion service at the Albert Hall where he had recited a verse from Laurence Binyon's poem "For the Fallen."

"They shall not grow old, as we that are left grow old ;
Age shall not weary them, nor the years condemn.
At the going down of the sun and in the morning
We will remember them."

Then he caught the night train for Portland, arriving at 4 o'clock in the morning, awaking three hours later to find that his railway carriage was standing in a foot of water on a storm lashed quay.

It seemed that the King's visits to his Navy were always doomed to be carried out in the most atrocious weather. When at 9 o'clock he entered his car at the station he asked : "Has it been fitted with floats ?"

Intimate contact with his Navy

On board the aircraft carrier H.M.S. Courageous more than a thousand men were drawn up, with the rain pelting down on their heads, and as the King came up on to the flight deck it was suggested that he should put on his waterproof. "Don't worry about me," he said, "but the men are getting soaked. Can't you get them under cover ?" In H.M.S. Nelson, where His Majesty in his capacity as Admiral of the Fleet, had been piped on board by the bo'sun, the King spent over an hour below chatting to the crew.

After a dinner party in the Royal Yacht, the King returned to the Courageous to attend a concert given by the lower deck. The hangar of the ship had been converted into a great hall and some 2,000 men drawn from every ship in the fleet were present to act as hosts to the Royal guest.

Except for the King and his suite no officers were allowed to attend.

The concert lasted for two hours, and was a typical lower-deck show.

MEDITERRANEAN HOLIDAY

Going ashore from yacht Nahlin at a Dalmatian port

"I want to congratulate you on this very enjoyable entertainment. It's a great pleasure to me to have this opportunity of visiting the Home Fleet before you disperse to your home ports for leave and refitment," he told them in a speech.

"As a matter of fact, I have a great feeling for Portland, because I left the Navy here as a midshipman — I will not say how many years ago—and I haven't actually been aboard a ship moored in Portland Harbour since that time. To-day, my times as a midshipman, when I served as an active officer, came back vividly to me.

"Ships' companies of the Home Fleet have been away in the Mediterranean for many months and in rather a difficult situation, I know. But you have all, shall I say, played the game extremely well. It is like a kind of welcome back to your home port on this occasion.

"As one who was brought up in the Navy, I am sure you will always do what we have been brought up to do. I wish you all a very good leave."

They cheered him.

Next day he continued his inspection of his Navy, and left with the traditional signal : "Splice the main brace !"

Which meant rum all round.

KING EDWARD RETURNING TO HIS
YACHT FROM THE ISLAND OF RAB

HOLIDAY FREEDOM IN DALMATIA

SHORE EXCURSION WITH MRS. SIMPSON

BATHING IN THE ADRIATIC

King Edward and Mrs. Simpson push boat into bathing
beach at Dubrovnik

KING EDWARD
AND MRS. SIMPSON
ON ADRIATIC ISLAND OF RAB

GOING ASHORE

AT SALTZBURG, AUSTRIA

KING EDWARD—OARSMAN

CHAPTER SEVEN

"Seeing for himself" in South Wales. A call at desolate Dowlais affects the King deeply. His Ways-and-Means discussion. "Something must be done. . ."

FIVE days later the King left London on a two-day visit to the South Wales Distressed Area, accompanied by Mr. Ernest Brown, Minister of Labour, and Sir Kingsley Wood, Minister of Health. A special train which left Paddington on Wednesday evening arrived at Llantwit Major at 5.30 in the morning, and the King breakfasted on the train before beginning his tour.

His first call was at the Boverton Co-operative Farm, where an archway of leeks had been erected by the miner-settlers.

"Arrange to send some of these leeks to London for me. I am very fond of them," he told the farm manager.

He asked one of the men the meaning of a numbered badge he was wearing. The man explained that the figure indicated his number on the pay-roll, and that everyone at the farm wore an identification disc.

"It is necessary, sir, for us to have numbers, for if you shouted out for Jones, twenty-five men would run towards you, and if you shouted for Davies you would have over thirty."

"And which are you—Jones or Davies?" laughed the King.

"I am Albert Jones," answered the man.

A Wartime memory

From Boverton, the King went to Dinas, where he inspected a parade of some 1,500 unemployed ex-Servicemen from the Rhondda Valley.

Then at Pentrebach he visited a social centre where training courses were given to unemployed men. Most of the men were at lunch when he arrived, but they dropped their knives and forks and stood to attention when the figure of the King appeared in the doorway.

Rapping sharply on the galvanized iron side of the hut, and addressing the men in the manner of an orderly officer, the King said: "Any complaints?"

Tremendous laughter greeted this inquiry.

While chatting with the cook—an ex-Naval man—at the Pentrebach centre, the King noticed that some of the men who had been in the middle of their lunch when he arrived were still on their feet. Interrupting his talk with the cook, he said, "Go on, sit down, your dinner will get cold."

Then, while driving through Merthyr Tydfil, he learnt that a number of Old Contemptibles were lined up in one of the streets. He at once gave orders that his car should be stopped, and in the narrow street, almost mobbed by thousands of townspeople, he inspected the ex-Soldiers.

From Merthyr the King went to Dowlais, one of the blackest districts in the area, and one which was not originally on the itinerary: the visit had been a last minute addition at the King's request.

Across the stone front of a cottage a message had been placed: "This town is poor but loyal." Above it fluttered a little Union Jack which had been tacked to a broom handle.

BACK FROM A PARTRIDGE SHOOT
King Edward, in Styrian costume, at a
holiday shoot in Lower Austria.

The King looked at it rather sadly and for a moment he was emotionally distressed.

Dusk had fallen before the sixty-mile tour ended at Mountain Ash, where a reception had been organized in the King's honour at the Pavilion. After listening to a choir singing the National Anthem, the King walked round the hall shaking hands and talking to the people in the crowd.

Throughout the first day of his tour, the King had been obviously affected by what he saw—the lean faces of the workless men, the misery and squalor in which they lived, and above all, the genuine enthusiasm with which thousands of helpless, broken-down families had greeted him everywhere.

WEARING THE BALMORAL TARTAN
King Edward and the Duke of York at Balmoral.

At Dowlais, as he stood gazing down at the ruins of what had once been a great and flourishing steelworks, employing 8,000 men, his eyes had been blinded by tears.

"These people were brought here by these works. Some kind of employment must be found for them," the King had said as he stood looking at the crowd grouped around the derelict works.

Despite his obvious fatigue, the King went straight from the Pavilion at Mountain Ash to his railway coach at Usk, there to discuss with Mr. Malcolm Stewart, the former Chief Commissioner for Special Areas, whom he had summoned on his own account, and Sir George Gillett, his successor, ways and means of alleviating the distress which he had witnessed.

The second day of the King's tour was largely a repetition of the first. A fifty-mile drive took His Majesty from Cwmbran, whither he had travelled by train from Usk, to Pontypool, Blaenavon, Brynmawr, Blaina, Abertillery and Rhymney. At each point along the route he was given a vociferous reception.

Visiting a junior instructional centre at Pontypool, he noticed that there was frosted glass in a window separating the "boys" and the "girls" sections.

"I see you want to keep their minds on their work," was his comment—typical of his light-hearted badinage.

Later, entering the cookery department at the same centre, he was told that the carrots and other vegetables were cooked by the "conservative" method so as to preserve their valuable mineral properties.

Turning to Mr. Arthur Jenkins, the Labour M.P. for Pontypool, the King remarked : "I should take notice of that if I were you."

At Blaenavon, the King was chatting to the Chairman of the local Council when he was told that the Monmouthshire hunger marchers—who had recently spent three weeks tramping to London to protest against the Means Test—were distributing an open letter, addressed to him, in the streets.

The King asked for a copy and put it in his pocket.

Several times during his visit he had said : "Something must be done, something will have to be done."

Who could have dreamed that a few days later the storms were going to break over his head ?

HIS FIRST PARLIAMENT OPENED
King Edward, surrounded by Heralds and Pursuivants,
preparing to leave House of Lords.

ARMISTICE DAY, 1936

King Edward greets his mother

28

WITH "THE MEN WHO REMEMBER"
At British Legion Remembrance Festival, Albert Hall

The History of The Abdication

The Bishop of Bradford speaks. Ten tense days of drama begin. Mrs. Simpson leaves for France. The King's "final and irrevocable decision."

CHAPTER EIGHT

TUESDAY, December 1st, 1936, saw the beginning of a ten-day drama of heroic proportions.

Its causes were long maturing, but the crisis was brought to a head with paralysing swiftness.

The curtain rose on the first act with an address on the forthcoming Coronation ceremony by the Bishop of Bradford. His listeners were his diocesan conference, but his words carried around the world. Two sentences only need be quoted—two sentences which were dropped like a lighted match into a cask of gunpowder. "We hope that King Edward VIII," said the Bishop, "is aware of his need to commend himself to the Grace of God.

"Some of us wish that he gave more positive signs of his awareness."

That was all. But a challenge had been given and was swiftly accepted by several of the leading provincial newspapers in England. London news organs at first maintained their long and self-imposed silence, but in the provinces the bishop's remarks were regarded as bringing to a head the gossip which, for several months, had connected the King's name with that of Mrs. Ernest Simpson, an American lady, who had divorced her first husband and had only a few weeks before secured a decree nisi in a petition against her second.

The national reserve having thus been broken down, the

London morning papers on the following day gave the public its first authoritative statement on the matter which had long occupied the attentions of the foreign press and caused uneasiness in the minds of responsible people in this country.

The situation was described as a "constitutional crisis," and despite the Prime Minister's disavowal that any constitutional difficulty existed, the feeling was widespread both in this country and in the Dominions that a grave crisis was, indeed, at hand.

❋ ❋ ❋

It was as long ago as 1920 that Mrs. Simpson first saw the then Prince of Wales. They were both at a naval ball at San Diego but they did not meet. King Edward first saw Mrs. Simpson when she was presented at Court in 1926, altho' it was eight years before they became close friends. From 1934 onwards, however, Mrs. Simpson and King Edward were constant companions. That year Mrs. Simpson was to be seen with the then Prince of Wales during his holiday at Biarritz, and the following year she was again his holiday companion.

Rumours in America

When he acceded to the Throne, King Edward made it clear that his feelings towards Mrs. Simpson were rather more than those of mere friendship; and American papers were beginning to discuss the affair openly and at considerable length.

The English public first saw Mrs. Simpson's name in print on May 28th—four months after the accession—when she appeared in the Court Circular as a dinner-party guest of the king.

To millions of British subjects throughout the world this announcement would have meant nothing ; but to several informed thousands in this country it was a cue for wild conjecture.

The King continued to act quite openly where Mrs. Simpson was concerned. Her name began to appear frequently in the Court Circular, and she was his guest at Buckingham Palace on several occasions.

Then came the Mediterranean cruise on the yacht Nahlin,

when the party, as we have seen, included Mrs. Simpson. Although Fleet Street was inundated with informal photographs of King Edward and Mrs. Simpson taken during the holiday cruise it was generally agreed not to publish them. The newspapers of this country continued to show respect for what it considered to be the private life of the Monarch ; it refrained from raising issues which it might never be necessary to raise. The wisdom of such a policy may be questioned, but not the motive which inspired it.

In the U.S.A., however, the newspapers gave great publicity to King Edward and Mrs. Simpson.

Rumours in England

Stories circulated in the American papers gradually reached the ears of certain influential members of the public in England. Conservative statesmen viewed the friendship with increasing alarm. The Prime Minister, Mr. Baldwin, became oppressed by the flood of rumours and comment and by the certainty that the wise silence of the home Press could not be indefinitely continued in the absence of a quiet solution.

The Prime Minister interviews the King

It was on October 20th, that the Prime Minister decided that it was his duty to speak to the King of his anxieties. He acted without consulting any of his colleagues. There was no question of the Prime Minister putting pressure on the King ; he merely offered a timely warning to His Majesty —a warning which was received in the spirit in which it was given.

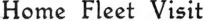

Home Fleet Visit

King Edward boards submarine Narwhal

This was the only occasion on which the Prime Minister pressed for an interview : so much for the belief that the King was being harassed by his Ministers.

A week later Mrs. Simpson obtained a decree nisi in her divorce suit at Ipswich. The case was quietly reported in the British Press, but without comment. To the Prime Minister, however, the event was the cause of added concern.

The King suggests abdication

On Monday, November 16th, the King sent for Mr. Baldwin. The latter set before His Majesty his view of a possible marriage. He said that he did not think that a particular

MEN OF H.M.S. ROYAL OAK

Inspected by King Edward on his visit to Home Fleet

WALES KNOWS HOW TO CHEER
King Edward, touring the depressed areas of South Wales, enters private home for a chat.

marriage was one that would receive the approbation of the country. He pointed out that such a marriage would involve the lady in question becoming Queen.

At the end of the interview the King said : "I am going to marry Mrs. Simpson, and I am prepared to go." It was on this note that the Prime Minister took leave of His Majesty, and did not see the King again until Wednesday, November 25th.

Compromise ?

On their next meeting, the King asked the Prime Minister whether a suggestion had been made to him that a com-

promise might be arranged to avoid the possibility of Mrs. Simpson becoming Queen. The compromise was that the King should marry and that Parliament should pass an Act enabling the lady to be the King's wife without occupying the position of Queen.

Mr. Baldwin told the King that such a proposition had been put to him, but that he had not considered it. If His Majesty were to ask for his first reaction informally, he said, his feeling was that Parliament would never pass such a Bill.

A week later the King once more sent for the Prime Minister. He asked him whether he was then in a position to give his considered opinion on the question which had been put to him. Mr. Baldwin stated that his enquiries had gone far enough to show that neither in the Dominions nor in this country would there be any prospect of such legislation being accepted.

Open discussion

This was how matters stood when the British newspapers first made public the relations which existed between King Edward and Mrs. Simpson, following upon the words spoken by the Bishop of Bradford. To the vast majority of

AT DERELICT STEEL-WORKS, SOUTH WALES

British subjects throughout the world the news came as a complete surprise. To those who had listened to the rumours and gossip which had been freely circulating on the other side of the Atlantic, the announcement came rather as a relief. But while the matter could now be openly discussed no one dared to offer a possible solution.

Questions in Parliament

On December 3rd, the day on which the general public became aware of the crisis, Mr. Attlee, the Opposition Socialist leader, asked the Prime Minister in the House of Commons whether any constitutional difficulties had arisen and whether he had any statement to make. Mr. Baldwin replied : "I have no statement to make to-day. While there does not at present exist any constitutional difficulty, the situation is of such a nature as to make it inexpedient

daily press, in the shops, in theatres and restaurants, and on every street corner in the country. We read that the King had summoned to Fort Belvedere three members of his entourage—and, incidentally, three of his closest friends ; of dispatch riders leaving Buckingham Palace with important papers for the King ; of the Duke of York's visit to the King ; of the Prime Minister's visit immediately afterwards ; of meetings of Ministers at Downing Street and in the Houses of Parliament. And all the time the country, in a frenzy of impatience, waited to hear that their worst fears were ungrounded.

Mr. Baldwin's statement

On Friday, December 4th, Mr. Baldwin made a statement in the House of Commons. It was a historic statement, and one which helped to clear the air, although it did little

A talk with Ex-Service Men, South Wales

that I should be questioned about it at this stage."

The House broke into cheers when Mr. Winston Churchill called for an assurance that no irrevocable step would be taken before a formal statement had been made to Parliament. The Prime Minister said that he had nothing to add to the statement he had already made. What he did not say, and what he could not say, was that the King had repeatedly said to him, during their private talks, "You and I must settle this matter together ; I will not have anyone interfering."

The topic of the day

There followed days of uncertainty, of anxiety, of confusion. The newspapers reported every movement of the Prime Minister and of the Cabinet. Hitherto unpublished pictures of King Edward and Mrs. Simpson appeared in every newspaper. Spain's plight, Hitler, Stalin, Mussolini—all were forgotten. Every item of news was read and re-read, examined from every angle by a bewildered public. From first to last the feeling of suspense was reflected in the

to lessen the anxiety of the people. The Prime Minister said : "*Suggestions have appeared in certain organs of the press yesterday and to-day that, if the King marries, his wife need not become Queen. These ideas are without any constitutional foundation.*

"*There is no such thing as a morganatic marriage known to our law. The Royal Marriages Act of 1772 has no application to the Sovereign himself. Its only effect is that the marriage of any member of the Royal Family is null and void unless it has the Sovereign's consent declared under the Great Seal. This Act, therefore, has nothing to do with the present case.*

"*The King himself requires no consent from any other authority to make his marriage legal, but, as I have said, the lady whom he marries, by the fact of her marriage to the King, necessarily becomes Queen. She herself, therefore, enjoys all the status, rights and privileges, which both by positive law and by custom, attach to that position, and with which we are familiar in the case of her late Majesty Queen Alexandra and Her Majesty Queen Mary, and her children would be in the direct line of succession to the Throne.*

WELCOMED TO MONMOUTHSHIRE

King Edward in flag-lined street at Abertillery,
November, 1936.

The only possible way in which this result could be avoided would be by legislation dealing with a particular case. His Majesty's Government are not prepared to introduce such legislation. Moreover, the matters to be dealt with are of common concern to the Commonwealth as a whole. Such a change could not be effected without the assent of the Dominions. I am satisfied from enquiries I have made that this assent would not be forthcoming.''

Mrs. Simpson leaves England

While the Prime Minister was making this statement to a crowded, expectant House, Mrs. Simpson, the woman who was causing an Empire to tremble—nay, to rock on its very foundations—was speeding across France to an unknown

would be among my passengers and was surprised when I learnt that she was on board. I am very sorry but I am instructed by the authorities not to reveal the name of the secretary, detective and chauffeur who were with her. They took two cabins.''

At 2.30 Mrs. Simpson and her party reached the Hotel de la Poste at Rouen. They were travelling in a large black saloon car which had been driven down to Newhaven from London before Mrs. Simpson's arrival at the port. As they entered the lounge of the hotel Mrs. Simpson was recognised by a French actress who next morning sent the news to Paris

From Rouen the car set off towards Paris. Until late in

"GRAVE ISSUES"
Newspaper posters in London, December 3, 1936

destination. As early as Thursday it was rumoured that Mrs. Simpson contemplated going abroad, but it was not until Saturday morning that it was known that she had slipped out of the country. This is how the story of one of the most dramatic and romantic flights in history was received in London on Saturday morning :

On Thursday night Mrs. Simpson escaped through the throng of curious watchers outside her house in Regent's Park, jumped into a police car which started at once for Newhaven. Two Scotland Yard officers formed an escort.

At Newhaven Mrs. Simpson, accompanied by an unidentified man, a detective, and a chauffeur, went on board the cross-channel steamer. This account of the voyage was given to the "Daily Express" over the telephone from Dieppe by the Captain of the vessel : "I was not warned that Mrs. Simpson

the afternoon the French police refused to make any statement. Then they admitted that Mrs. Simpson was in France and said they had been instructed to observe the greatest secrecy about her visit.

—still travelling

Five o'clock brought the news that Mrs. Simpson had lunched at Evreux, and had then passed through Dreux and Chartres. Arrival at Chartres was taken as an indication that Mrs. Simpson was making for the Riviera, and the next report was that she was going to Cannes to stay with Mr. and Mrs. Herman Rogers, old friends who had been guests of the King during his holiday cruise in the yacht Nahlin during the summer. This proved true; and it was at this villa that Mrs. Simpson spent the weeks of the crisis and afterwards.

A week-end of suspense

This, then, was how matters stood when the people of the Nation went home for their week-ends. A meeting of the Cabinet had been held on Saturday morning at which the Prime Minister had reported on his fifty-minute interview with the King at Fort Belvedere the previous evening. No statement was forthcoming, but it was announced that the Cabinet would meet again on Monday morning. It was further understood that a definite move would be made within the next forty-eight hours. But despite promises and assurances, the dreaded word "abdication" began to loom in the minds of everyone in the country.

Public Opinion

On all sides opinions began to be freely and forcefully expressed. One heard the question being asked : "Why shouldn't the King marry the woman he loves?" And such phrases as "the dignity of the Crown," "the disruption of the Empire," "devotion to duty" were bandied about. But from the highest to the lowest in the land the sympathy went out to the unhappy Monarch in his terrible dilemma, and in no less a degree to his mother, Queen Mary, who was suffering such distress.

**Mr. BALDWIN
LEAVING No. 10 TO
VISIT KING EDWARD
AT "THE FORT"**
December 5, 1936

(Right)
**AT THE GATES,
FORT BELVEDERE**

Sunday, December 6th, 1936, will be remembered as one of the most ominous in our history. The drama of the day touched many places—Downing Street, where the Cabinet met twice ; Fort Belvedere, Marlborough House, Queen Mary's home ; Buckingham Palace, where crowds stood all day ; *Lou Viei*, the villa in Cannes.

In the afternoon on Monday, December 7th, the Prime Minister made another statement in the House of Commons. The statement which was made in identical terms in the House of Lords by Lord Halifax, was as follows :

"In considering this whole matter it has always been, and remains, the earnest desire of the Government to afford to His Majesty the fullest opportunity of weighing a decision which involves so directly his own future happiness and the interests of all his subjects. At the same time they cannot but be aware that any considerable prolongation of the present state of suspense and uncertainty would involve risk of the gravest injury to national and Imperial interests, and indeed no one is more insistent upon this aspect of the situation than His Majesty.

"In view of certain statements which have been made about the relations between the Government and the King, I should add that, with the exception of the question of morganatic marriage, no advice has been tendered by the Government to His Majesty,

**ARMY DESPATCH RIDER FROM
"THE FORT" AT "No. 10"**

with whom all my conversations have been strictly personal and informal. These matters were not raised first by the Government, but by His Majesty himself, in conversation with me some weeks ago, when he first informed me of his intention to marry Mrs. Simpson whenever she should be free.

"The subject has, therefore, been for some time in the King's mind, and as soon as His Majesty has arrived at a conclusion as to the course he desires to take he will no doubt communicate it to his Governments in this country and the Dominions. It will then be for those Governments to decide what advice, if any, they would feel it their duty to tender to him in the light of his conclusion.

"I cannot conclude this statement without expressing—what the whole House feels—our deep and respectful sympathy with His Majesty at this time."

On a previous occasion in the House of Commons, when a member had got up to question the Prime Minister on the crisis, he had been greeted by cheers. This time, both before and after his statement, Mr. Baldwin had the sympathy and understanding of the entire House. There was no support for Mr. Churchill, who attempted a speech in the form of a supplementary question and was forced to resume his seat by jeering cries. Nor was there anything but applause for the curt negative with which Mr. Baldwin dismissed an earlier question.

Mrs. Simpson's attitude

On Tuesday, December 8th, a statement was given to journalists at Cannes by Lord Brownlow, a Lord-in-waiting to His Majesty, who was with Mrs. Simpson.

"Mrs. Simpson," it said, "throughout the last few weeks, has invariably wished to avoid any action or proposal which would hurt or damage His Majesty or the Throne.

"To-day her attitude is unchanged, and she is willing, if such action would solve the problem, to withdraw forthwith from a situation which has been rendered both unhappy and untenable.

"Mrs. Simpson has given no interview of any sort or kind, has made no statement whatsoever, other than the statement I now make on her behalf."

This news was received with mixed feelings. But such was the readiness of the public to snatch at a straw that it was

Ascot, June, 1935

King Edward, then Prince of Wales, with Mrs. Simpson.

at once interpreted as at least offering hope of a happy solution of the constitutional crisis. The news from Cannes reached the House of Commons about five hours after Mr. Baldwin had first mentioned Mrs. Simpson's name in the House.

Anxiety in the Colonies

But the crisis was not over; rather was the suspense increased when it became known that Mr. Baldwin had paid the King another visit at Fort Belvedere. Wednesday morning's newspapers spoke of the deep concern felt in India, of Australian anxiety, of the injury of prolonged suspense felt by the people of South Africa. A Cabinet meeting was promised for Thursday morning, at which the Prime Minister would report to his colleagues the latest phase of the situation. Mr. Baldwin had dined with the King on the occasion of his last visit, and the Duke of Kent—who was with His Majesty all Tuesday afternoon—and the Duke of York—who had spent several hours with the King on Monday night—were also present at dinner that night.

The hours slowly dragged on. The people formed in queues to buy their newspapers; switched on their wireless sets at all hours of the day, hoping to learn of some definite move. There was only one topic of conversation, one question on everybody's lips: Would King Edward, the man who had served his people so well for the best years of his life, the man who had endeared himself to countless millions all over the world, decide to abdicate?

How could such a thing be allowed to happen?

Never before in the history of the British Throne had a King voluntarily abdicated. Surely such a catastrophe could be avoided in these enlightened days?

The Final Crisis

At last the stage was set for the final scene. On Thursday, December 10th, it was announced in the press that a message from His Majesty the King, to Parliament, giving His Majesty's decision on the questions which had been occupying his anxious attention and that of his Ministers for over a week, would be read in the House of Commons by the

Daily Express

TODAY'S WEATHER : MILDER.

RADIO PROGRAMMES: PAGE 23.

ONE PENNY

TUESDAY, DECEMBER 8, 1936

No. 11,409

Mrs. Simpson Authorises
Dramatic Statement From Cannes

I AM WILLING TO WITHDRAW
If Such Action Would Solve The Problem

LORD BROWNLOW READS SIGNED DOCUMENT

'A Situation Which Has Become Both Unhappy And Untenable'.

Daily Express Staff Reporter

CANNES, Monday Night.

Mrs. Simpson is "willing, if such action would solve the problem, to withdraw forthwith from a situation that has been rendered both unhappy and untenable."

Her offer is made in a statement signed by Mrs. Simpson herself which Lord Brownlow, Lord-in-Waiting to and close friend of the King, read to a Press Conference in the Hotel Majestic, Cannes, tonight. The statement said:—

"Mrs. Simpson, throughout the last few weeks, has invariably wished to avoid any

Mrs. Simpson

DAILY EXPRESS
FRONT PAGE STORY FROM CANNES

Prime Minister that afternoon. A similar statement would be made in the Lords.

From an early hour there was every indication that the sittings of the two Houses of Parliament that day would be one of the most dramatic of recent times—not even excluding the period which preceded the Great War.

It was at a quarter to three that the Speaker took the Chair in the House of Commons. The House was crowded to its utmost limits : there was only one vacant seat on the front benches—that of the Prime Minister who did not enter the House until shortly after 3.30.

There were fifty-one questions on the order paper and these had to be disposed of before the main business of the day could be begun. The Prime Minister entered while the questions—many of them of the mildest order—were in progress. He was loudly cheered by members in all parts of the chamber. The tension, which had been steadily growing, now reached its height. Yet there was no attempt to curtail the ordinary questions ; indeed there was a note of nervous flippancy as the questions were spun out to occupy the time until the pre-arranged minute.

The King's message

At precisely 3.42 Mr. Baldwin rose, amid a general cheer,

39

and strode down the House to the Bar. He turned about, bowed low to the Speaker, Captain Fitzroy, and, raising the fateful document which he held in his right hand, said : "A message from His Majesty the King, signed by His Majesty's own hand."

The Prime Minister then advanced to the table, passed to the left of it and, bowing again immediately in front of the Chair, handed the paper to the Speaker. Members wearing hats uncovered their heads in sign of respect. A deep silence fell upon the House as the Speaker, Captain Fitzroy, holding the document in hands which trembled, began to read out the King's message :

"After long and anxious consideration, I have determined to renounce the Throne to which I succeeded on the death of my father, and I am now communicating this, my final and irrevocable decision. Realising as I do the gravity of this step, I can only hope that I shall have the understanding of my peoples in the decision I have taken and the reasons which have led me to make it. I will not enter now into my private feelings, but I would beg that it should be remembered that the burden which constantly rests upon the shoulders of a Sovereign is so heavy that it can only be borne in circumstances different from those in which I now find myself. I conceive that I am not overlooking the duty that rests on me to place in the forefront the public interest when I declare that I am conscious that I can no longer discharge this heavy task with efficiency or with satisfaction to myself.

"I have accordingly this morning executed an Instrument of Abdication in the terms following :

"I, Edward VIII, of Great Britain, Ireland, and the British Dominions beyond the Seas, King, Emperor of India, do hereby declare my irrevocable determination to renounce the Throne for myself and my descendants, and my desire that effect should be given to this Instrument of Abdication immediately.

"In token whereof I have hereunto set my hand this tenth day of December, nineteen hundred and thirty-six, in the presence of the witnesses whose signatures are subscribed."

(Signed) EDWARD R.I.

DECEMBER 6, 1936 : THE ARCHBISHOP OF CANTERBURY VISITS MR. BALDWIN

"My execution of this Instrument has been witnessed by my three brothers, their Royal Highnesses the Duke of York, the Duke of Gloucester, and the Duke of Kent.

"I deeply appreciate the spirit which has actuated the appeals which have been made to me to take a different decision, and I have, before reaching my final determination, most fully pondered over them. But my mind is made up. Moreover, further delay cannot but be most injurious to the peoples whom I have tried to serve as Prince of Wales and as King and whose

They Flocked to Downing Street

Seeking news of King Edward . . . December 3rd, 1936

future happiness and prosperity are the constant wish of my heart."

"I take my leave of them in the confident hope that the course which I have thought it right to follow is that which is best for the stability of the Throne and Empire and the happiness of my peoples. I am deeply sensible of the consideration which they have always extended to me both before and after my accession to the Throne and which I

Newspaper men at No. 10

know they will extend in full measure to my successor.

"I am most anxious that there should be no delay of any kind in giving effect to the Instrument which I have executed and that all necessary steps should be taken immediately to secure that my lawful successor, my brother, his Royal Highness the Duke of York, should ascend the Throne.'"

(Signed) EDWARD R.I.

Changing of the Guard, Buckingham Palace, December 4th.

LONDON CABARET, 1936

Mrs. Simpson, guest of King Edward, just before he came to the Throne

The message was received in silence. And in a silence equally solemn the Prime Minister rose to make his speech. "Sir, I beg to move that His Majesty's most gracious Message be now considered."

It was a speech which by its simplicity succeeded where rhetoric would have surely failed.

The complete story

The story began in mid-October, when Mr. Baldwin returned to "half-time" work after his holiday. He found at once a flood of correspondence from British subjects all over the world expressing uneasiness at the tales in the American press, and he himself was disquieted by the knowledge that Mrs. Simpson's divorce suit was imminent. He decided that it was a duty, which could only fall on the Prime Minister, to warn the King as a counsellor and friend. On Sunday, October 18th, therefore, without consulting any of his colleagues (an omission for which they had forgiven him) he asked for an interview—the first and only time when the initiative had come from him.

WINTER SPORT, AUSTRIA, 1935

With Mrs. Simpson : off to the ski-ing slopes of Kitzbühel

MRS. SIMPSON

The meeting took place at Fort Belvedere on October 20th; and Mr. Baldwin prefaced his account of it by an illuminating revelation of the consistent attitude of the King and of himself. He himself had taken the line that a servant was useless unless completely frank; and the King had never taken offence at anything thus frankly said.

Consideration for the Crown

On October 20th, Mr. Baldwin told the King of the prevalent gossip, reminded him that, though the Crown had lost many of its prerogatives, the importance of preserving its integrity was greater than ever before, and observed that the present respect for the Crown, built up during three generations, might be destroyed far more rapidly than it had been built up. He expressed the desire that these criticisms should have no cause to continue, recalled the bright hopes he had entertained of the new reign, and offered to help as a friend. He also pointed out the danger of the impending divorce case.

Mr. Baldwin then left the King to consider these observations, reported them to four of his senior colleagues, and felt relieved that the ice was broken.

On Monday, November 16th, the King sent for the Prime Minister at Buckingham Palace. At that meeting Mr. Baldwin spoke to His Majesty about a possible marriage for about twenty minutes. Since their last meeting a decree nisi had been pronounced in the divorce case, and the Prime Minister told the King that marriage with Mrs. Simpson could not meet with public approval, that the King's wife must be Queen and therefore in his choice the voice of the people must be heard. "I may be a remnant of the Old Victorians," Mr. Baldwin had said, "but my worst enemy would not say of me that I did not know what the reaction of the English people would be to any particular course of action."

Mr. Baldwin went on to say that the King then told him something which he had long wanted to tell him. He said: "I am going to marry Mrs. Simpson, and I am prepared to go."

DEMONSTRATION IN WHITEHALL, DECEMBER 10th, 1936

Mr. Baldwin replied that this was grievous news, and that he must withhold comment. That same night the King told Queen Mary, and his brothers were told during the next two days.

Morganatic marriage considered

The third meeting was on November 25th. On that occasion the King had asked Mr. Baldwin about the compromise suggestion of a morganatic marriage. He asked the Prime Minister what he thought about it. Mr. Baldwin replied that in his view Parliament would never pass the necessary Bill. But the King wanted the matter examined formally, and, though warned that it meant consultation with the full Cabinet and the Dominion Prime Ministers, expressed the desire that this should be done.

On December 2nd, Mr. Baldwin reported the results of his inquiries. The King did not seem surprised at the answer—the only formal decision of any kind so far taken by the Cabinet—and he behaved like a great gentleman, never referring to the matter again. At this interview the Prime Minister told him plainly what the alternative appeared to be—namely, either to abandon his project or to abandon his Throne in the hope of later contracting his marriage if that were possible.

HURRYING HOME

The Duke of York—December 4th.

The King's Problem

During the next week the King was left to continue the struggle alone. Mr. Baldwin asked the House to remember that His Majesty was not a boy, that although he looked so young he was a mature man with wide and great experience of life and the world; and he wanted to emphasize that the King had always before him four considerations, which he had repeated again and again : that if he went he would go with dignity ; that he wanted to go with as little disturbance to his Ministers and his people as possible ; that he wished to consider his brother in every possible way ; that any idea to him of a "King's party" was abhorrent. The King had remained at Fort Belvedere because he said he was not going to come to London while these things were in dispute, thus giving opportunity for popular demonstrations.

Mr. Baldwin then produced a pencilled note which he had that morning received from the King. It said : "Duke of York—he and the King have always been on the best of terms as brothers and the King is confident that the Duke deserves and will receive the support of the whole Empire."

"Where I have failed," said Mr. Baldwin, "nobody could have succeeded ; and those who know the King know what that means."

MRS. SIMPSON : A STUDIO PORTRAIT

THE LAST PHASE

Fort Belvedere, night of December 10th, 1936.

So Mr. Baldwin came to the last date in his story—December 9th. In the morning the Cabinet received the King's formal decision. They replied, in a minute which Mr. Baldwin read out, expressing their profound regret and urging that he should change his mind even now. But all was in vain, and the King refused to alter his decision.

"None of us," said Mr. Baldwin, "will want to judge him: we are not judges."

The last act of the Ministers

The duty of Parliament was now to close their ranks and do what the King wished. Therefore he appealed for dignity and swift action upon the Bill to be passed on the following day, for restraint and for special thought for "the revered and beloved" Queen Mary.

At the conclusion of the Prime Minister's speech the sitting of the House was suspended, and the shortest reign in 453 years of English history was in its last few hours. With a stroke of the pen, next day, December 11th, Edward Albert Christian George Andrew Patrick David, Edward VIII, of Great Britain, Ireland, and the British Dominions beyond the Seas, King, Emperor of India, had handed over his Throne to his brother.

King Edward's Farewell

King Edward VIII said his farewell to the nation in a 537-word speech over the radio on the same night of the eleventh. And not only the nation, but all the world listened to his words. Never in the world's history had a speech been delivered to an audience so immense. Never before has a royal voice carried such human poignancy to the four corners of the earth.

At 10 p.m. the burry voice of Sir John Reith, Director-General of the B.B.C., came over the air. "This is Windsor Castle—His Royal Highness Prince Edward."

There was a pause, and a shock ; Prince Edward !

Then the man who had been our King began to talk, clearly, slowly, in balanced tones, without passion—while the world listened.

46

INSTRUMENT OF ABDICATION

I, Edward the Eighth, of Great Britain, Ireland, and the British Dominions beyond the Seas, King, Emperor of India, do hereby declare My irrevocable determination to renounce the Throne for Myself and for My descendants, and My desire that effect should be given to this Instrument of Abdication immediately.

In token whereof I have hereunto set My hand this tenth day of December, nineteen hundred and thirty six, in the presence of the witnesses whose signatures are subscribed.

SIGNED AT
FORT BELVEDERE
IN THE PRESENCE
OF

Edward RI

Albert

Henry.

George.

A REIGN ENDED

Instrument of Abdication, signed by King Edward and his three brothers.

The Farewell Broadcast Speech

"At long last I am able to say a few words of my own. I have never wanted to withhold anything, but until now it has not been constitutionally possible for me to speak.

"A few hours ago I discharged my last duty as King and Emperor, and now I have been succeeded by my brother, the Duke of York, my first words must be to declare my allegiance to him. This I do with all my heart.

"You all know the reasons which have impelled me to renounce the Throne. But I want you to understand that in making up my mind I did not forget the country or the Empire which, as Prince of Wales and lately as King, I have for twenty-five years tried to serve.

"But you must believe me when I tell you that I have found it impossible to carry the heavy burden of responsibility and to discharge my duties as King as I would wish to do without the help and support of the woman I love.

"And I want you to know that the decision I have made has been mine and mine alone. This was a thing I had to judge entirely for myself. The other person most nearly concerned has tried up to the last to persuade me to take a different course. I have made this, the most serious decision of my life, only upon the single thought of what would in the end be best for all.

"This decision has been made less difficult to me by the sure knowledge that my brother, with his long training in the public affairs of this country, and with his fine qualities, will be able to take my place forthwith without interruption or injury to the life and progress of the Empire, and he has one matchless blessing enjoyed by so many of you and not bestowed on me, a happy home with his wife and children.

"During these hard days I have been comforted by Her Majesty my mother and by my family. The Ministers of the Crown, and in particular Mr. Baldwin, the Prime Minister, have always treated me with full consideration.

"There has never been any constitutional difference between me and them, and between me and Parliament.

"Bred in the constitutional tradition by my father I should never have allowed any such issue to arise.

"Ever since I was Prince of Wales, and, later on, when I occupied the Throne, I was treated with the greatest kindness by all classes of my people wherever I have lived or journeyed throughout the Empire.

"For that I am very grateful.

"I now quit altogether public affairs, and I lay down my burden.

"It may be some time before I return to my native land, but I shall always follow the fortunes of the British race and Empire with profound interest, and if at any time in the future I can be found of service to His Majesty in a private station I shall not fail.

"And now we all have a new King. I wish him, and you, his people, happiness and prosperity with all my heart.

"God bless you all !

"GOD SAVE THE KING !"

Then all broadcasts ceased for the night, and the man who had been our King slipped away from Windsor Castle—where he had spoken this epic farewell—and hurried through the night into exile. At 1.50 the destroyer, H.M.S. Fury, slipped out of Portsmouth harbour bound for Boulogne.

A day later Edward, Duke of Windsor, was in Vienna on his way to Castle Enzesfeld as the guest of the Rothschild family.

> "I give this heavy weight from off my head,
> And this unwieldy sceptre from my hand,
> The pride of kingly sway from out my heart.
> With mine own tears I wash away my balm.
> With mine own hands I give away my crown.
> With mine own tongue deny my sacred state.
> With mine own breath release all duty's rites."
>
> "Richard the Second."

✻　　　✻　　　✻

PRINCE EDWARD
Leaving Windsor Castle after his moving broadcast to the Empire

From the book by Michael Chance, published by John Murray. Photograph by Studio Lisa

The Happy Family

The King and Queen with their daughters, Elizabeth and Margaret Rose, and some of the Princesses' pets.
The Queen is in "Y Bwthyn Bach" (The Little House), gift of the people of Wales to Princess Elizabeth.

King George VI

Ascends the Throne

Early training at Osborne and Dartmouth. Under fire at Jutland. Mentioned in dispatches. He wins his pilot's wings. "The Industrial Prince." The King's sympathy with youth.

CHAPTER ONE

NO sovereign in British history ever ascended the Throne in quite such circumstances of poignancy and drama as Albert Frederick Arthur George, on December the tenth, 1936.

The day had broken bleakly over London, as if the tremendous events of the past week had cast their shadow on the capital. People were still stunned by the series of shattering blows which had assailed everything that they held most dear and the farewell words of the man who had been their King still echoed in millions of minds. A cloak had been torn aside that shelters not only sovereigns but the humblest of their subjects in love, and the family of British peoples felt the blaze of critical publicity as keenly as would any smaller family—and, as any smaller

An indication of a career-to-be :
Sailor-suited Prince Albert.

King George VI, as a baby, with
his mother. He was born at
York Cottage, Sandringham, on
December 14, 1895.

From Babyhood to Youth

Left : Still sailor-suited—
Prince Albert at the age of six.

Right : Aged sixteen—
Prince Albert, Naval cadet at
Osborne.

THE CHILDREN OF KING GEORGE V AND QUEEN MARY

At Balmoral : Prince George (Duke of Kent), Prince Albert (King George VI), Princess Mary (The Princess Royal), Prince Edward (now Duke of Windsor), and Prince Henry (Duke of Gloucester). *Absent* : Prince John, youngest son, who died in 1919.

family, clung the more closely together in this moment of crisis.

So, while the man who had been King Edward the Eighth sped across Europe to his exile, the machinery of Empire leapt into movement and George the Sixth was proclaimed King, by the Grace of God, of Great Britain, Ireland and the British Dominions beyond the Seas, Defender of the Faith, Emperor of India.

Royal Proclamation

In London the ancient ceremony conformed to tradition, and on that cold December afternoon the proclamation was read at St. James's Palace, at Charing Cross, Temple Bar and the Royal Exchange. But it was not until the story of

the Empire's proclamations began to arrive that the air of national depression lifted.

For this crisis had been a crisis of Empire ; it was the first test of the Act of Westminster which five years before had made the King of England also the King of Canada, the King of Australia, King of South Africa and King of New Zealand— each Dominion independent not only of the other but of Great Britain itself.

And these invisible bonds had stood the test ; not one link (save possibly the Free State, on Britain's very doorstep, which chose to phrase its political attitude with character- istic wealth of paradox) was weakened. Indeed, the result of this constitutional crisis was to strengthen Imperial unity. Thus, swept on and encouraged by the great pageant of

Prince Albert (*second from left, inside brake*), arrives at Devonport to board the cruiser Cumberland which took him to the West Indies, Canada and Newfoundland.

Naval cadet Prince Albert in the Royal Yacht Victoria and Albert, 1912.

Empire loyalties, the people's minds turned to the man whom destiny had placed upon the Throne.

They knew him as a serious, conscientious Royal Duke, with many of the graver virtues possessed by that other illustrious prince after whom he had been christened; and who—like that Prince Consort—enjoyed an obviously happy married life, with a charming wife and two children. But a natural desire for privacy had enabled him to keep somewhat out of the limelight which shone so much more brightly on his elder brother, and, indeed on his own wife and children.

Albert Frederick Arthur George, second son of his Majesty King George the Fifth and of Queen Mary, was born on December 14, 1895, in York Cottage, Sandringham.

It was the anniversary of the death of Prince Albert, Queen Victoria's consort.

The childhood days of Prince Albert were spent in the company of his elder brother, the then Prince Edward, and of his sister Princess Mary, all three being born within three years of each other.

The two Princes played football with the village boys at Sandringham, they played cricket, shot, rode, and even had lessons in golf. Fishing and stalking were two other sports which both Royal princes took up at an early age.

The Girl who became The Queen

At the age of two : the Lady Elizabeth Angela Marguerite Bowes-Lyon.

A studio portrait of Queen Elizabeth as a child

Fancy Dress. Glamis Castle. Aged Nine.

Lady Elizabeth Bowes-Lyon as a young girl

Bridesmaid at wedding of Princess Mary and Viscount Lascelles (now the Princess Royal and the Earl of Harewood). February 28th, 1922.

There is a story that the King once performed the hat-trick at cricket, bowling in turn his grandfather, his father, and his brother. The ball with which he performed this feat was afterwards to be seen as a trophy at Osborne when the King returned there. When their parents were abroad on Empire engagements, the three children were looked after by their grandfather and grandmother, King Edward and Queen Alexandra. It was, in fact, a custom even when the family were together for the young Princes and Princess Mary to pay King Edward a visit every evening—visits which King Edward himself came to enjoy as much as his grandchildren.

The occasion of these visits soon came to be looked upon as providing an opportunity for such rough and tumble ragging that Mr. Hansell, the Princes' tutor, was ordered by an anxious mother to accompany the children and see that they behaved properly.

The young Prince was educated for the Navy, and if boyhood drawings mean anything, a naval, or at any rate an engineering, career was of his own choosing.

ENGAGED

Tennis party, 1923 : The Duke of York and Lady Elizabeth Bowes-Lyon.

WEDDING DAY. APRIL 26th, 1923

Lady Elizabeth Bowes-Lyon leaving her London home to become a British Princess.

MARRIED IN WESTMINSTER ABBEY

The Duke and Duchess of York are kneeling at the Altar. In the Royal group are Queen Alexandra, King George V, and Queen Mary.

There is a picture, drawn in coloured chalks when he was 7, which depicts a pump magically pouring forth a flood of water and flying the flag of a full admiral! One assumes that the pump was of a nautical design, although its construction and method of operation appeared highly problematical.

Shortly after his fourteenth birthday, Prince Albert was sent to Osborne to begin his naval training in earnest. He went in as an ordinary cadet with no privileges or marks of rank. Among the subjects which he studied were mathematics, physics, electricity, engineering, French, English composition and literature, general naval history, navigation and seamanship. Although he applied himself thoroughly to his studies he did not distinguish himself, except in seamanship.

Examinations, as he confessed later, found him "usually at the bottom of the list."

His ability to handle a boat better than most of his year, however, is shown by the impatience with which he used to watch the efforts of his elder brother—who had entered Osborne a year ahead of him.

BRIDE AND BRIDEGROOM
Acknowledge cheers, after their wedding, from the balcony, Buckingham Palace.

ROSE-PETAL SHOWER
Leaving the Palace on their honeymoon

ROYAL HONEYMOON

The Duke and Duchess of York strolling through the wooded grounds of
Polesdon Lacey, Surrey, where the first part of their honeymoon was spent.

THEIR FIRST DAUGHTER
The Duke and Duchess of York with the Princess Elizabeth, born on April 21st, 1926.

But he could not very well openly make fun of the Prince of Wales, who was a senior cadet.

Sixteen months after he had entered Osborne, the reign of King Edward the Seventh came to an end. Together the two cadet Princes, Edward and Albert, marched solemnly in the funeral procession behind the new King, their father, the German Kaiser, and the Duke of Connaught. But while Prince Edward had now become heir-apparent, with new duties and responsibilities suddenly thrust on his young shoulders, for Prince Albert there yet remained the serious business of making himself an efficient naval officer, and he returned to Osborne to continue his studies.

The prince remained at Osborne for two years, and then entered the Naval College at Dartmouth. His general record there, as well as at Osborne, was one of which any man might well be proud. He never sought the limelight, nor did he ever attempt to evade his responsibilities; he worked as he played, quietly but with determination.

The Prince passed out of Dartmouth in December, 1912. He was then just seventeen years old. Shore training over, he went aboard H.M.S. Cumberland, a county cruiser of 9,000 tons, to find his sea legs in the usual six-months' cruise. It was in the Cumberland that the King had his first glimpse of the outside world, visiting Teneriffe, St. Lucia, Trinidad, Barbados, Martinique, Dominica, Porto Rico, Jamaica, Havana, Bermuda, Canada and Newfoundland.

There was one incident which occurred in Montreal which showed that the naval Prince could enjoy a joke—and share it with others—as cheerfully as anybody.

The occasion was a dance given in his honour, and the host had been at great pains to select suitable partners for the Prince from the ranks of the leading citizens.

EAGER TO SEE THE BABY PRINCESS
Crowd rush Royal car as it Leaves Buckingham Palace after the christening of Princess Elizabeth Alexandra Mary. May 29th, 1926.

ROUND-THE-WORLD TOUR BEGINS

Farewell Kiss from the Prince of Wales on deck of the battleship Renown. January 6th, 1927. The Duke
and Duchess of York were leaving on voyage which took them to Australia and New Zealand.

HONOUR FROM A "KING"

The Duchess of York invested with the "Order of the Golden Mermaid" by King Neptune at Crossing the Line ceremony in the Renown. The Duke looks on, laughing.

PARTNERS

A game of deck tennis in the Renown

When the dancing began, however, the Prince showed an inclination to dance with partners other than those specially chosen for him.

The Commander—knowing the host's exertions—tried to get the right partners forward when, as a result of his energetic chaperoning, both the buttons at the back of his trousers came adrift.

The Prince soon heard of the Commander's dilemma, considered the unfortunate episode too good to keep to himself.

For from that moment onwards there was no further talk of any partners being neglected. The Prince danced with everyone he possibly could, each of his partners in turn being told of the Commander's predicament.

From a somewhat doubtful beginning, the function quickly became a huge success—that is, if one ignores the feelings of the unhappy Commander.

On his return home to England, Prince Albert became a midshipman aboard H.M.S. Collingwood, then flagship of the

A DUCKING TO FOLLOW . . .

The Duke, lathered and "shaved" by Neptune's men, Crosses the Line in the Renown first battle squadron. At the outset he made it clear that he wished to be treated as an ordinary member of the ship's company; and it wasn't long before Prince Albert became plain Mr. Johnson to his shipmates. Even ratings sometimes addressed the Royal midshipman as "Mr. Johnson."

War broke out not long after the Prince had taken up his duties in the Collingwood. A month later he became ill and was rushed ashore for an appendicitis operation. After convalescence he was sent for service in the Admiralty, and it was not until early in 1915 that he rejoined his ship.

In the following year illness once again sent him back to the Admiralty; but he was able to return to the Collingwood in time for the battle of Jutland, and it was here that he first came under fire.

The Collingwood began to shell German destroyers and the Derfflinger. The Prince's station was in a fore turret and he carried out his duties so thoroughly that he even served up the usual cocoa to his turret mates. For his work he was mentioned in Admiral Lord Jellicoe's dispatches, and one of his mementoes of the occasion is the white ensign the Collingwood flew during the historic engagement.

ARRIVING AT LAS PALMAS CANARY ISLANDS

January 10th, 1927.

With a catch at Tokaanu, New Zealand.

WADING A NEW ZEALAND STREAM

Early morning fishing expedition, Tongariro River, North Island.

BIG GAME FISHING, BAY OF ISLANDS, NEW ZEALAND

The Duke lands a ground shark.

TWENTY FISH IN HALF AN HOUR

The Duchess of York fishing from a motor-boat in the Bay of Islands, New Zealand. One of the twenty fish she caught in thirty minutes was this schnapper.

The Duke secures his ground shark to stern of motor-boat, Bay of Islands.

After the battle of Jutland, the Prince spent a good deal of time aboard hospital ships. He suffered continually from gastric trouble and finally, after a period as acting-lieutenant aboard H.M.S. Malaya, he went ashore and underwent an operation for duodenal ulcer.

It was soon apparent that his naval career was over.

Despite his willingness to carry on, his constitution at that stage did not fit him for a life at sea. In February, 1918, therefore, he went to the Royal Naval Air Station at Cranwell, to be one of the first naval officers to be absorbed into the Royal Air Force when the naval arm and the Royal Flying Corps were combined.

And in October, 1918, the Prince crossed to Nancy where he served on the air staff of Sir Hugh Trenchard.

A Royal Representative

The Armistice came, and shortly afterwards the Prince went on his first official mission on behalf of his father, representing King George at the spectacular entry of King Albert of the Belgians into Brussels.

The Prince returned to England in February, 1919, and five months later won his pilot's wings. As an example of his quiet determination never

The Sister Princesses

to shirk responsibilities, he went up for his final test despite having been strongly advised to postpone the attempt on account of the bad weather.

"I can't have the thing hanging over my head," was all that he said before facing the ordeal ; then he went up and passed the test.

Social Work

After a brief period at Trinity College, Cambridge, where he took a house with his brother, then Prince Henry, instead of going into residence in the College, he began specializing in social and industrial work. While his elder brother and heir to the Throne voyaged about the world as Britain's "ambassador of good-will," Prince Albert went among his fellow-countrymen studying industrial conditions at home.

It was not so much duty, this, as natural inclination

While he was always eager to talk with people of all classes, his natural reserve did not allow him to make friends very easily. But while he may not have had the human touch which came so readily to his elder brother, his determination to probe deeply into every problem and to see for himself the conditions of life in various parts of the country made people appreciate his earnestness.

His Marriage to Lady Elizabeth Bowes-Lyon

On April 26, 1923, Prince Albert, now Duke of York—he had been created Duke of York in 1920—was married to Lady Elizabeth Angela Marguerite Bowes-Lyon, daughter of the Earl and Countess of Strathmore and Kinghorne, their engagement having lasted little more than three months.

Although the romance was then termed "a simple, old-fashioned love match," it was not such a simple affair for the Duke.

The Earl of Strathmore has since told us that the Duke had proposed three times to his daughter before she finally accepted.

There was no modern precedent for the marriage of a commoner with a Royal Prince so close to the Throne in the line of succession. The marriage, however, was widely acclaimed, and the Royal Family fully approved the union.

Queen Mary, with whom the new Duchess became increasingly popular, said of her daughter-in-law "She is not one of these modern girls, thank Heaven."

The Bride

The Duke of York's bride was born on August 4, 1900, at the family's English seat, St. Paul's Waldenbury. Apart from two terms spent in a day school in London, she was educated entirely at home. She studied music, learned to become a good needlewoman, practised cooking, and engaged in the outdoor life of a well-bred gentlewoman.

She once, dressed as a maid, showed a group of American tourists over Glamis Castle, the grim and stately seat of the Strathmores in Scotland.

The new Duchess had always avoided extremes. In her dress she was inclined to be colourful in a nice conservative way ; "Betty blue" was the smart colour of 1924. Blue-eyed, dark haired, with a charming smile for every one, she soon captured the hearts of the nation.

Yet until her engagement to the Duke in January, 1923, she was unknown to the public, and even Mayfair knew her little.

The Duke's Public Engagements

With a wife at his side to give him confidence and encouragement, the man who was one day to be King George the Sixth, plunged into a fuller and more arduous life with increased energy.

He visited factories and industrial centres, coming into contact with some of the richest, as well as some of the humblest, men in the land.

He became the "industrial Prince," founded the "Duke of York's Camp" (a development of the Industrial Welfare Society whose president he was, and whose work he described as "cementing that fellowship between individuals in all walks of industry irrespective of class or occupation which is the backbone of our Imperial programme").

Interest in Youth Organisations

In the camp he annually brings, or did up until last summer, together for a fortnight's holiday, 200 factory boys and 200 boys from various public schools.

His attitude towards the youth of the country has always been genuine and sympathetic.

Children of the poorer classes began to look to him as the guardian of their play-grounds, and in 1925 he became president of the National Playing Fields Association, an organization formed to provide adequate play-grounds for children.

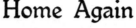

Home Again

The Duke and Duchess landing at Portsmouth, June 27, 1927. Behind them are the Prince of Wales, the Duke of Gloucester and the Duke of Kent.

—AND HE FORGOT HIS HAT!

Young courtier, presenting a purse at Child Welfare garden party,
St. James's Palace, made—and marred—a magnificent bow.

When the King "shot" the Shooters

King George VI, as Duke of York, was photographed, *left*, at his 1932 camp at Southwold with some of his boy guests from public schools and industrial areas.

Afterwards he asked Press photographers a number of questions about the working of their cameras.

"That's all right," he said. "You fellows are always photographing me. Now I'll show you what it feels like. Line up! . . ."

The picture below was taken with the borrowed camera.

"I'll just take one more—in case," the Duke said, quoting the photographer's formula, so familiar to him.

Some days later, he said to a Press photographer who had been in the group: "I see that photograph I took appeared in the newspapers."

His Guests—and Future Subjects

The Duke of York watching boys' sports on
the foreshore, New Romney camp, 1927

Film-maker

Making a cinema record at one of his annual camps for boys.

69

ROYAL ENGINE-DRIVER

The Duke of York at boys' camp (held annually from 1921 to 1929 at
New Romney, Kent) drives miniature train.

The story is told of two lads who presented themselves bright and
early one morning at the Duke's London home at 145 Piccadilly, and
asked to see His Royal Highness.

A policeman barred the way and questioned the boys on the nature of
their mission ; tearfully, they explained that their cricket pitch had
been appropriated for some public purpose and "what," they asked
naively, "is the Duke going to do about it ?"

They did not go away disappointed ; he did something about it.

Royal Ambassador

The Duke's first Empire trip was his journey to East Africa in 1924-5.

There, in addition to hunting big game, he visited a number of native
chiefs and came into contact with members of the Administration ; he
was accompanied on that trip by the Duchess.

Back in England again he continued to apply himself to his official duties
with quiet efficiency.

OFF FOR A DIP

Although first and foremost the Duke was always regarded as a family man, he frequently visited the Continent as his father's representative and—at one time or another—he has seen nearly all the European capitals.

But between his East African trip and his voyage to Australia to open the new Parliament buildings at Canberra on May 7th, 1927, his time was largely taken up with domestic affairs.

Princess Elizabeth

On April 21, 1926, the Duchess gave birth to her first child, Princess Elizabeth Alexandra Mary, the little child who, by the time she had reached the age of 10, was to become the most important girl in the world.

The brief career of Princess "Lilibet" is almost too well known to bear repeating. She and her little sister, Princess Margaret Rose, who was born on August 21, 1930, are known to millions.

Golden-haired, blue-eyed, fair-complexioned, she has long enjoyed the distinction of being the most photographed young lady in the land.

Her studies begin each day at 9.30 in the morning and continue until noon. In the afternoon she is taken out for a drive, or plays games with Margaret Rose and their few friends. At the Royal Lodge in Windsor Great Park, her parents' country home, she has her own garden, her dogs, and a pony.

She loves dogs—so does Princess Margaret Rose—and has eight of them for her constant companions: four retrievers, two Welsh corgis, a spaniel and a Tibetan lion dog.

Each year she is made to knit scarves for her Royal grandmother's "Needlework Guild" and the scarves (dropped stitches and all) are given to poor people.

So far the Princess has had only one really important public appearance. That was when she acted as a very efficient

QUEEN MARY—GRANDMOTHER

A picture taken at Sandringham in January, 1936, with the Princesses Elizabeth and Margaret Rose and Prince Edward, son of the Duke and Duchess of Kent.

The Times Copyright

(amazingly so) bridesmaid for her uncle, the Duke of Kent, at his marriage to Princess Marina, of Greece. But she has been seen by thousands of Londoners riding in the Row in Hyde Park, or playing in the gardens behind 145 Piccadilly. And London loves her.

The Duke and Duchess' tour of Australia and New Zealand in 1927 proved a great success and showed that, despite

Princess Elizabeth Heir Presumptive

AT THE AGE OF NINE

ONE YEAR OLD

A PICTURE POPULAR ALL OVER THE WORLD

Elizabeth

FIRST PICTURE TAKEN WITH HER MOTHER: MAY, 1926

1930 : SHE CALLED HERSELF "PRINCESS LILIBET" THEN

72

Princess Margaret Rose

TWO YEARS OLD

PORTRAIT TAKEN LAST YEAR

A THIRD BIRTHDAY STUDY

Margaret Rose

FOURTH BIRTHDAY:
AUGUST 21, 1934

FIRST PICTURE TAKEN WITH HER MOTHER: OCTOBER, 1930

"OVER THE SEA TO SKYE"

Landing in storied Skye from the yacht Golden Hind, 1933. On the hill
across the bay, at Kyleakin, are the ruins of Castle Maoil.

THE CRYPT, GLAMIS CASTLE

the Duke's natural reserve and shyness, he could, when
necessary, conquer his diffidence.

A visit to an old friend

While he was visiting New Zealand, the Duke learnt that
Mr. Watt, his former tutor at Osborne, and the man who
taught him how to fish, was also on a visit to New Zealand.
Although he was in the middle of the tour he motored
several miles to talk over old times with him.

Like his father before him, the Duke never forgets to repay
a debt of gratitude.

As a sportsman, Britain's new King is a fair golfer (not
playing very much), a moderate shot, likes tennis and riding
to hounds. He swims, has played football, cricket and
squash, skated and fished. He is a good all-round sportsman;
he himself modestly says that he is just "a player of games."

Experts have credited him with having the quickest eye for
a ball in the family.

THE QUEEN AT HER OLD HOME
With the Princesses Elizabeth and Margaret Rose
at historic Glamis Castle.

THE HOME THAT WALES BUILT

Princess Elizabeth and "Y Bwthyn Bach" (The Little House)—gift of the people of Wales—in garden of Royal Lodge, Windsor.

With one of her dolls at the most famous Dolls' House in the world.

As a tennis player—a left-hander—he was good enough to compete at Wimbledon ; as a golfer he has been captain of a number of clubs, including the Royal and Ancient of St. Andrews.

But a favourite indoor sport of King George the Sixth is to relax in an armchair in front of the fire and read detective stories. And when mystery yarns have lost their appeal, he turns to books on hunting, shooting, and to biographies.

As an amateur photographer he had his own camera, projector and theatre, and recorded many incidents in the life of the Royal family ; there was even one occasion when he turned the tables on press photographers by getting behind the camera himself and shooting them with his cine.

—AND FRIENDS

The Princesses with some of their pets at Royal Lodge, Windsor.

From the book by Michael Chance, published by John Murray.   Photograph by Studio Lisa

PRINCESS ELIZABETH IN THE SADDLE

A ride in Windsor Great Park.

BIG OCCASIONS FOR SMALL PRINCESSES

Excited Princesses Elizabeth and Margaret Rose arriving at Olympia for the Royal Tournament, 1935 . . .
Princess Margaret, at the age of three, enjoying herself at a fete in Scotland . . . Princess Elizabeth,
hand outstretched, steps from her car to greet an officer.

CATCHING "BUBBLES"

The Duchess of York tries her luck at "bubble catching," Regent's Park garden party, 1931.

Painting, as such, has little attraction for him; he is a normal Englishman in his tastes, going dutifully to the Royal Academy to see the "pictorial" side of the show.

On one occasion he spotted a picture of the Duke of Connaught wearing the ribbon of the Order of the Garter over the wrong shoulder; and at another time he paused before a portrait of Napoleon by Jean Ingres and wanted to know why the wrong hand was thrust in the traditional pose into the jacket. "The buttons are also on the wrong side," he explained.

HIS GIFT

Shy young man had just presented bottle of sweets to the Duchess at charity gift day.

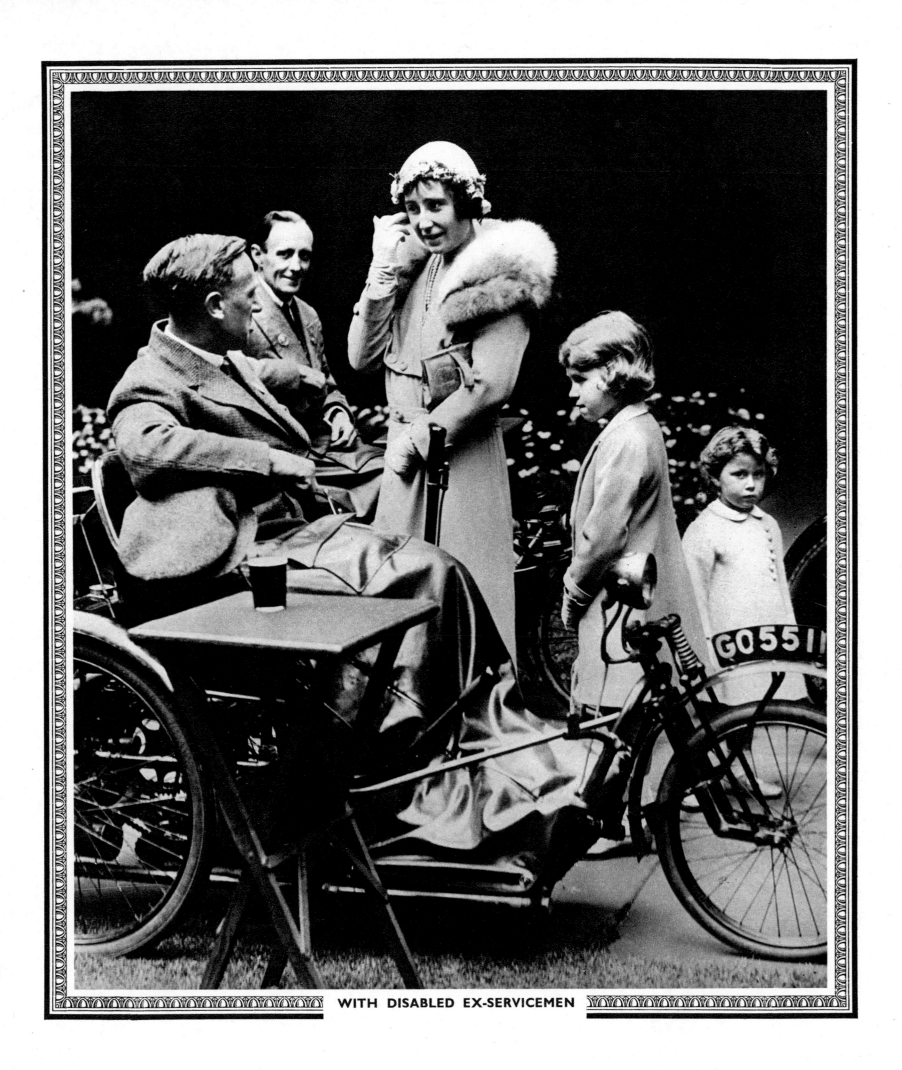

WITH DISABLED EX-SERVICEMEN

81

RINGSIDE

Watching Civil Service boxing championships, 1930.

SERVICE

The King (as Duke of York) played in the men's doubles at Wimbledon in 1926.

DRIVE

Playing for the Generals in a match against the Admirals.

Off to a Rally
of Scouts and Guides

NEW STAVES

Presentations at Hadfield rally of Girl Guides, 1931.

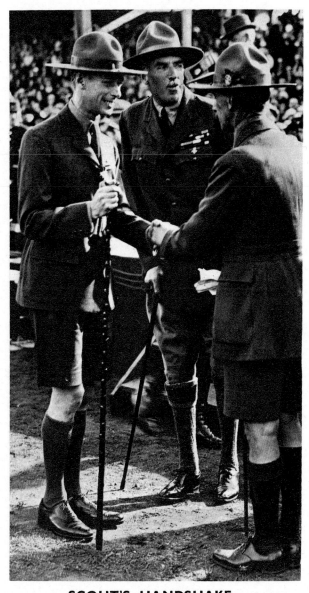

SCOUT'S HANDSHAKE

Rally at Adelaide, 1927. The then Governor of South Australia, Sir Tom Bridges, Chief Scout of the State, is next to him.

The Duke and Duchess leaving to attend a parade of 3,000 Boy Scouts and Girl Guides.

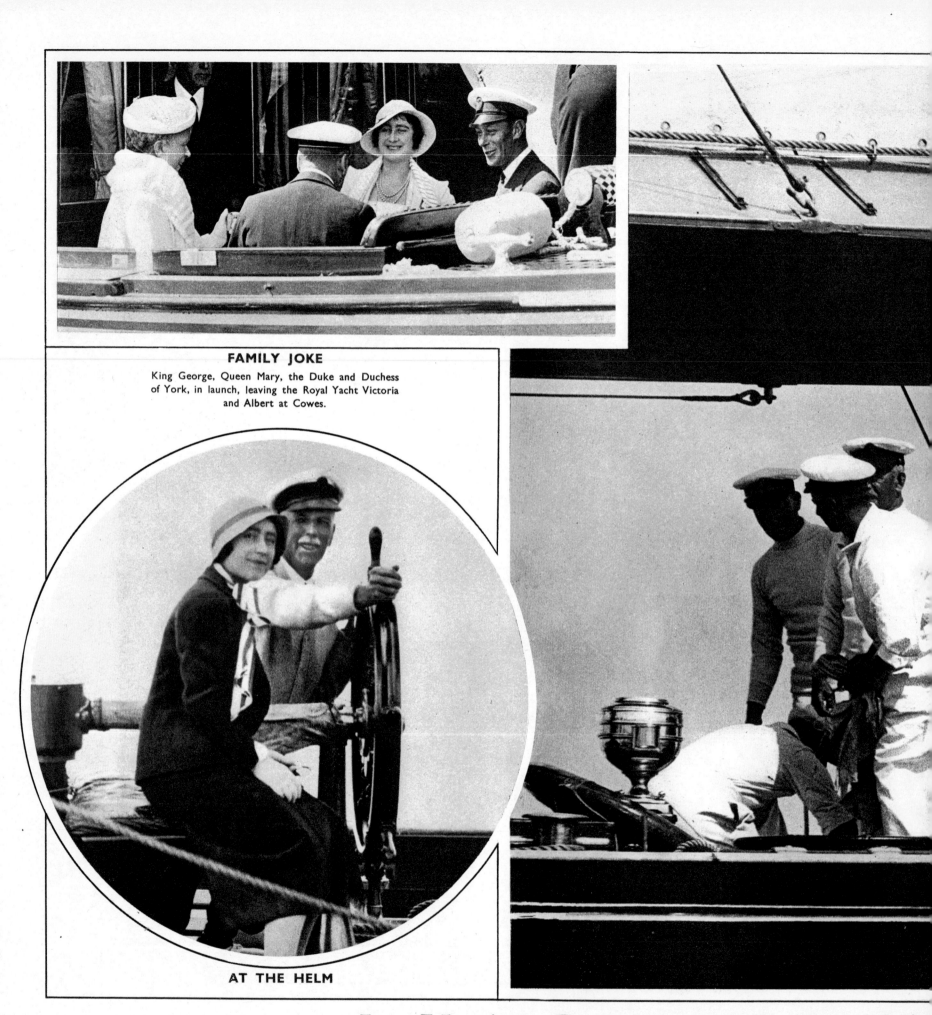

FAMILY JOKE

King George, Queen Mary, the Duke and Duchess of York, in launch, leaving the Royal Yacht Victoria and Albert at Cowes.

AT THE HELM

In Yacht Race round the Isle

of Wight

The Duke and Duchess of York were accompanying King George V
in the Britannia at Royal Thames Yacht Club Regatta, 1935

THE NEW REIGN DAWNS

The King, in Admiral's uniform, leaving No. 145 Piccadilly, to attend the Accession
Council at St. James's Palace, December 12, 1936.

Kings
of Arms
Proclaim
a King

Norroy King of Arms, in his richly-emblazoned tabard, reading the Proclamation of the Accession of King George VI at Chancery Lane, December 12, 1936. Following tradition, the procession of heralds and pursuivants had been halted at Temple Bar where Bluemantle Pursuivant demanded, in the ancient form, admission into the City. Order-in-Council requiring the Proclamation having been delivered to the Lord Mayor, the barrier was removed. Proclamation was read to citizens of London from the steps of the Royal Exchange (*top picture*) by Clarenceux King of Arms.

THE ROYAL FAMILY TREE

House of Windsor

KING GEORGE VI (1936—)	Married Lady Elizabeth Bowes-Lyon	Crowned May 12, 1937
KING EDWARD VIII (1936)	Abdicated December 10, 1936	Reigned eleven months
KING GEORGE V (1910-1936)	Married Victoria Mary of Teck	Britain's well-beloved

House of Saxe-Coburg

KING EDWARD VII (1901-1910)	Married Alexandra of Denmark	Man of the world, keen sportsman
QUEEN VICTORIA (1837-1901)	Married Albert of Saxe-Coburg	Crowned at 18, reigned 64 years
KING WILLIAM IV (1830-1837)	Married Adelaide of Saxe-Meiningen	Served 10 years in the Navy
KING GEORGE IV (1820-1830)	Married Caroline of Brunswick (refused admission to Coronation)	Gifted, but dissolute and extravagant
KING GEORGE III (1760-1820)	Married Charlotte of Mecklenburg-Strelitz	In this reign England lost the American colonies
KING GEORGE II (1727-1760)	Married capable, adroit Caroline of Ansbach	Ambitious of military glory. Niggardly, irritable
KING GEORGE I (1714-1727)	Married Sophia-Dorothea of Celle (a prisoner until her death)	Never learned the English language ; died in Hanover

House of Stuart

QUEEN ANNE (1702-1714)	Married George of Denmark. Her many children died young	Daughter of James II and Anne Hyde
KING WILLIAM III and QUEEN MARY II (1689-1702)	Reigned and crowned together as Joint-Sovereigns. Mary died in 1694	Prince of Orange. A fighter of courage. Made few friends
KING JAMES II (1685-1688)	Married twice	Fled to France, where he died
KING CHARLES II (1660-1685)	Married Portuguese princess, Catherine of Braganza	Brilliant, cynical. Knew defeat, exile, poverty
(Commonwealth declared 1649. Oliver Cromwell, Lord Protector, 1653-1658. Richard Cromwell, Lord Protector, 1658-1659)		
KING CHARLES I (1625-1649)	Married Henrietta-Maria of France	Executed at Whitehall
KING JAMES I (1603-1625)	Married Anne of Denmark	James VI of Scotland

House of Tudor

QUEEN ELIZABETH (1558-1603)	Saw England rise to be a First-class Power	Majestic daughter of Henry VIII and Anne Boleyn
QUEEN MARY I (1553-1558)	"Bloody Mary": married Philip of Spain	Embittered daughter of Henry VIII and Catherine of Aragon
QUEEN JANE (1553)	Executed at the Tower, aged 17	Reigned 14 days

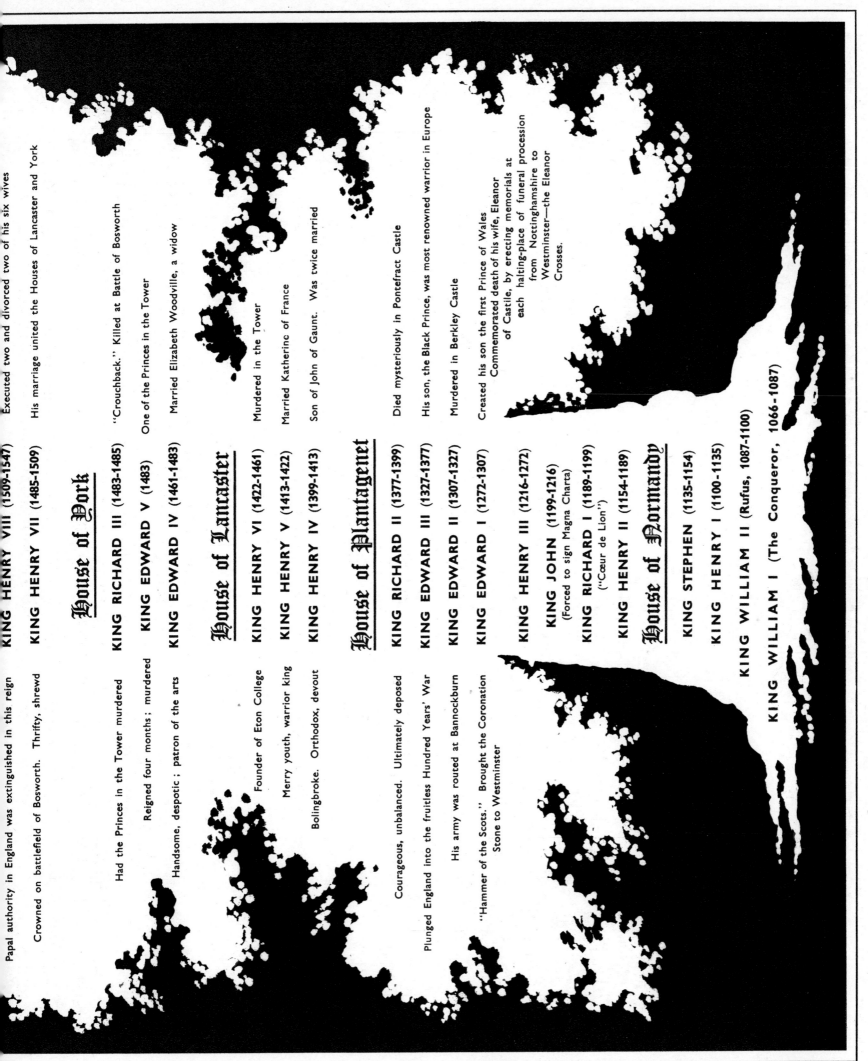

KING HENRY VIII (1509-1547) — Papal authority in England was extinguished in this reign / Executed two and divorced two of his six wives

KING HENRY VII (1485-1509) — Crowned on battlefield of Bosworth. Thrifty, shrewd / His marriage united the Houses of Lancaster and York

House of York

KING RICHARD III (1483-1485) — Had the Princes in the Tower murdered / "Crouchback." Killed at Battle of Bosworth

KING EDWARD V (1483) — Reigned four months; murdered / One of the Princes in the Tower

KING EDWARD IV (1461-1483) — Handsome, despotic; patron of the arts / Married Elizabeth Woodville, a widow

House of Lancaster

KING HENRY VI (1422-1461) — Founder of Eton College / Murdered in the Tower

KING HENRY V (1413-1422) — Merry youth, warrior king / Married Katherine of France

KING HENRY IV (1399-1413) — Bolingbroke. Orthodox, devout / Son of John of Gaunt. Was twice married

House of Plantagenet

KING RICHARD II (1377-1399) — Courageous, unbalanced. Ultimately deposed / Died mysteriously in Pontefract Castle

KING EDWARD III (1327-1377) — Plunged England into the fruitless Hundred Years' War / His son, the Black Prince, was most renowned warrior in Europe

KING EDWARD II (1307-1327) — His army was routed at Bannockburn / Murdered in Berkley Castle

KING EDWARD I (1272-1307) — "Hammer of the Scots." Brought the Coronation Stone to Westminster / Created his son the first Prince of Wales. Commemorated death of his wife, Eleanor of Castile, by erecting memorials at each halting-place of funeral procession from Nottinghamshire to Westminster—the Eleanor Crosses.

KING HENRY III (1216-1272)

KING JOHN (1199-1216) (Forced to sign Magna Charta)

KING RICHARD I (1189-1199) ("Cœur de Lion")

KING HENRY II (1154-1189)

House of Normandy

KING STEPHEN (1135-1154)

KING HENRY I (1100-1135)

KING WILLIAM II (Rufus, 1087-1100)

KING WILLIAM I (The Conqueror, 1066-1087)

Order of Succession. 1, Princess Elizabeth; 2, Princess Margaret Rose; 3, Duke of Gloucester; 4, Duke of Kent; 5, Prince Edward; 6, Princess Alexandra; 7, Princess Royal; 8, Viscount Lascelles; 9, The Hon. Gerald Lascelles; 10, Princess Arthur of Connaught; 11, Earl of Macduff; 12, Lady Maud Carnegie.

Crowd waiting outside No. 145 Piccadilly, hoping for a glimpse of the new King, Sunday, Dec. 13.

The Queen

Studio portrait taken soon after the Accession.

Leaving No. 3 Belgrave Square, home of the Duke and Duchess of Kent, for the christening of Baby Princess Alexandra at Buckingham Palace, February 9, 1937.

AND HOW THEY CHEERED..

The King at the Christ Church Boys' Club, Lambeth. He was visiting the Duchy of Cornwall estates in South-East London to mark the 600th anniversary of the granting of the charter of the Duchy of Cornwall to the Black Prince.

Early Days of The Reign

The King's first public duties. New assurance of manner. A visit to Aintree. The Queen's dignity and poise.

CHAPTER TWO

BY the time that King George the Sixth had ascended the Throne, his people already knew many of his kingly virtues.

It had been apparent early in his reign that the new monarch was setting his standards by those of his beloved father ; and many of the Court officials who had served King George V returned—or remained—to advise the new sovereign.

Few men have ever had to begin in such arduous and peculiar circumstances as those facing King George VI in the first five months of his reign ; all eyes were upon him ; and they were critical eyes.

His attitude became one of tact and modest discretion and for the first two months he scarcely appeared in public at all, and the daily Court Circular chronicled few activities. During that time he was, with characteristic thoroughness, learning all he could of the delicate machinery of the Palace in its relation to the State.

Royal Acknowledgments

But during February he knighted two men : one Mr. Walter Monckton K.C., and the other Mr. Eddie Marsh, the senior Private Secretary of the Civil Service and a man of varied accomplishments.

Then on February 13th—which was a Saturday—the new King and Queen made their first ceremonial appearance by driving through London to the East End.

CHRISTMAS MORNING, SANDRINGHAM, 1936

The King and Queen with their daughters and the Duchess of Gloucester on their way to Church.

SHARING A JOKE AT AINTREE

The King and Queen in Royal Box waiting for the start of the 1937 Grand National.

The occasion was the opening of the new People's Palace, and (as George V had found during his post-Jubilee drives) the streets were gaily decorated by the people themselves; Union Jacks and chalked words of welcome on the walls were evidence of the East End's traditional loyalty.

A Visit to the B.I.F.

Later in the month the King began the first of the public duties which had always appealed to the serious side of his nature as Duke of York : he visited the British Industries Fair at the White City.

No superficial visits, these, but exhaustive (and exhausting) tours of the miles of exhibits with his wife and mother ;

it was, indeed, his first big public appearance with Queen Mary.

The Grand National

A month later the King made his first provincial appearance at Liverpool, where he was cheered by vast crowds. With the Queen he had been the previous day to the Grand National with Lord Derby. Those who saw him at Aintree detected a new assurance in his manner, an absence of that diffident nervousness which had sometimes character-ised him as a younger man.

It was the old story of the man rising to the requirements of his job, of nature changing the human being instead of the human being trying to change the role which he had to

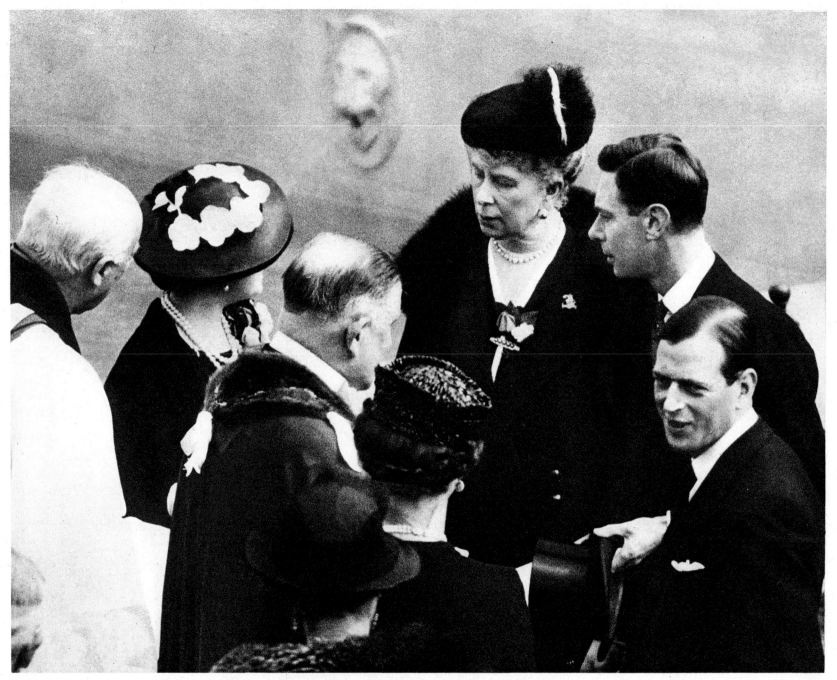

MEMORIAL TO HIS FATHER UNVEILED

The King with the Queen, Queen Mary, the Duke and Duchess of Kent and the Dean and Mayor of Windsor after the unveiling of the memorial, beneath the walls of Windsor Castle, to George V—first Sovereign of the House of Windsor, April 23, 1937.

play. History has many precedents.

Nor was the change confined to the King; for into the former Duchess of York's jolly manner had crept a becoming dignity and poise.

As the weeks slipped by and the now-historic events of May 12th came closer, the King retreated more and more from the public eye; much of his time was spent with his family at Windsor.

The King's busy life

But again the Court Circular had a tale to tell and it was evident that the King was even busier than ever. The period of rest which had been prescribed for him was denied by the demands of office. On some days he had individual audiences with as many as thirty people and saw as many as seventy more.

The Unveiling of Two Memorials
to the Memory of His Father

On April 20th, he unveiled the King George V Memorial at Wellington Barracks in the morning, and in the afternoon paid a surprise visit to the Court jewellers to try on the Imperial Crown of State; his head proved to be slightly larger than his father's.

Three days later, at the festival of St. George, he unveiled the Windsor Memorial to his father. Here he made his first public speech since his accession:—

The Royal Standard flew from an admiral's barge—escorted by four motor torpedo-boats—as it carried the King and Queen, with Princess Elizabeth, on a triumphal down-river progress for the opening of the National Maritime Museum at Greenwich. Queen Mary travelled by car to Greenwich; heard the King's speech in Neptune's Hall.

The Queen's Crown and Coat of Arms

A new design—the first British crown to have all the jewels mounted in platinum. Only diamonds are used, principal among them the Koh-i-Noor, set in a cross patée springing from the regal circlet. Half-crown in larger picture gives an indication of the size of this 106-carat gem.

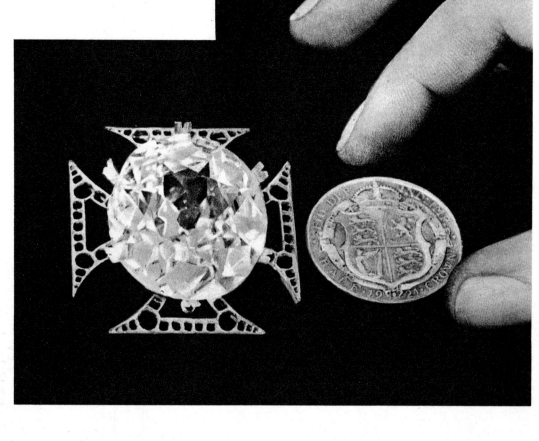

THE QUEEN'S COAT OF ARMS

The Shield carries the Royal Arms of England, "impaling" the Arms of the Queen's family. The Lyon quarters closely resemble the Scots Royal Arms. Dexter supporter is the Lion of England; sinister supporter, the Lion of Bowes-Lyon. Shield is encircled with the Garter and surmounted by the Royal Crown.

"If I may speak for a moment of him in whose honour this memorial has been erected, let me only say that to me, personally, the memory of my father will always bring the inspiration of a high example.

"I hope that in trying to fulfil our great responsibilities the Queen and I may be supported by some measure of that trust and affection which were so fully given to him and to my dear mother by the people of this country and of the Empire."

The Coronation

It was an exhausting period, but the King survived it triumphantly and when May 12th arrived, was able to sustain his burden as the central figure in the great pageant of the Coronation with assurance and dignity.

✳   ✳   ✳

Princess Elizabeth's Coronet

Of silver-gilt with jewel-like chasing mounted with fleurs-de-lis.

Princess Margaret's Coronet

Like that of Princess Elizabeth. Both are specially designed for lightness.

THE IMPERIAL CROWN
OF STATE

Made for Queen Victoria. Its gems include the second-largest portion of the Star of Africa; a sapphire from the crown of Charles II; the Black Prince's ruby; pearls believed to have been ear-rings of the Tudor Queen Elizabeth and a sapphire held to have come from a ring of Edward the Confessor.

THE IMPERIAL CROWN
OF INDIA

Made for King George V and with which he was crowned Emperor of India at Delhi in 1912. The Crown of England is by law, not allowed to be taken from the shores of Britain and a new crown was therefore designed for India.

THE CORONATION CHAIR AND THE
STONE OF SCONE

Under the seat of this chair is a rough lump of stone, sometimes called the Stone of Destiny, on which the ancient Kings of Scotland were crowned. It was carried away by Edward I who had the chair built to enclose it. Every sovereign of England since then, with the exception of Edward V, Mary I and Mary II, has been crowned on this seat.

THE SWORD OF STATE

Richly jewelled. Made for George IV at a cost of £6,000. Now worth many times that sum. Borne before the King in the Coronation procession.

THE AMPULLA OR GOLDEN EAGLE

Into this vessel is poured the consecrated oil with which the King is anointed at his Coronation. The oil is poured through the beak into the golden Coronation Spoon. The Archbishop of Canterbury, dipping his fingers into the spoon, anoints the King in the form of a cross on the brow, the breast and the palms of the hands. Ceremony takes place beneath a cloth-of-gold canopy held by four Knights of the Garter.

His Majesty King George VI

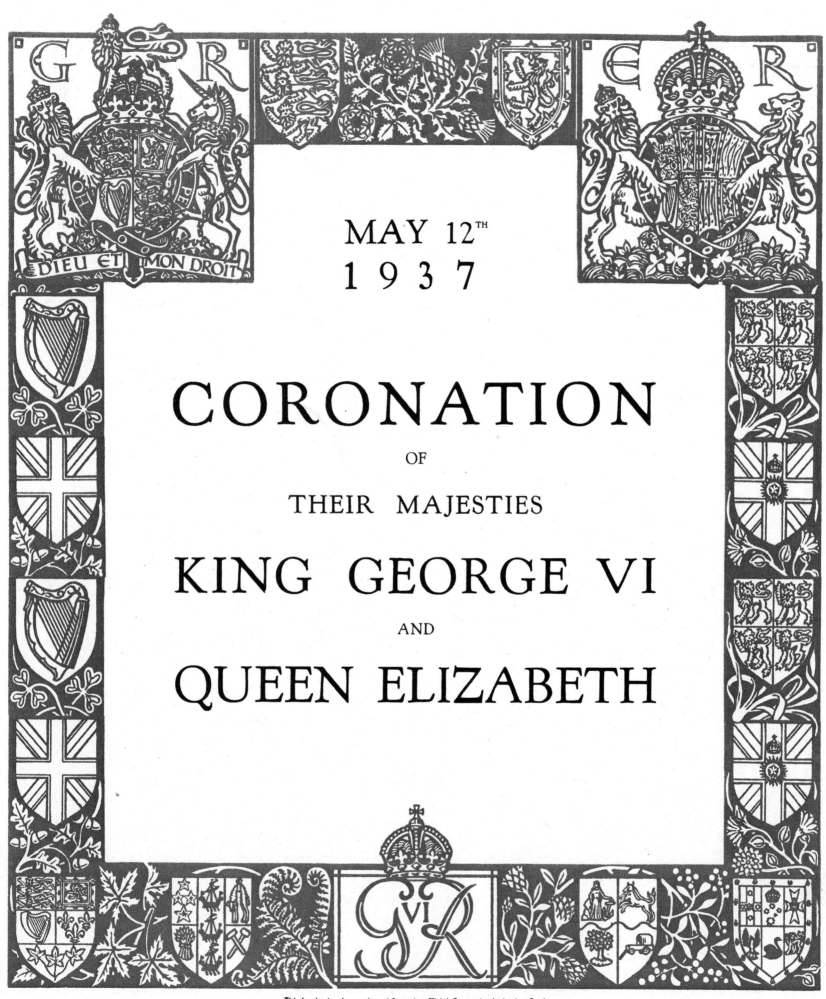

MAY 12TH
1937

CORONATION

OF

THEIR MAJESTIES

KING GEORGE VI

AND

QUEEN ELIZABETH

This border has been adapted from the official Coronation Invitation Card.

THE KING AND QUEEN LEAVE THE PALACE
FOR THEIR CORONATION

They rode in the great golden coach first used in 1762 by George III. A shaft of
sunlight—first of the day—fell on the coach as the eight greys entered the forecourt.

FANFARE OF TRUMPETS. ROLL OF DRUMS

"God Save the King" . . . A second of silence, then a thunder of cheers
from the packed stands as the Coronation Coach swung into view.

SWINGING DOWN THE MALL

The carriage procession of Prime Ministers, representatives of India and Burma and Colonial Rulers. Each carriage had its appropriate mounted escort. In this group were the Sultans of Zanzibar, Johore, Trengganu, Pahang ; the Yang Di-pertuan Besar of Negri-Sembilan ; the Amir of Transjordan.

AVENUE OF BANNERS

Each emblazoned with the arms of the King and Queen. The State Coach is followed
by a glittering Sovereign's escort.

Queen Mary, stately figure in her coach of glass, was accompanied by Queen Maud of Norway.

Princess Elizabeth and her cousin, Lord Lascelles, in the royal carriage-procession from the Palace. They were with the Princess Royal.

A Close-up of the

Coronation Coach

It is twenty-four feet long, weighs four tons and is supported at each corner by the figure of a Triton.

THE KING'S PERSONAL AIDES-DE-CAMP

Riding behind the Coronation Coach. *Left to right* : The Duke of Gloucester, the
Duke of Kent, the Earl of Athlone, Lord Louis Mountbatten.

STAND
53

THROUGH THE ADMIRALTY ARCH

SAILORS LINE THE ROUTE IN TRAFALGAR SQUARE

. . . AND SO INTO WHITEHALL

The King and Queen

pass The Cenotaph

THE EARL AND COUNTESS OF CADOGAN

LORD AND LADY ARMSTRONG

Peers and Peeresses at the Abbey

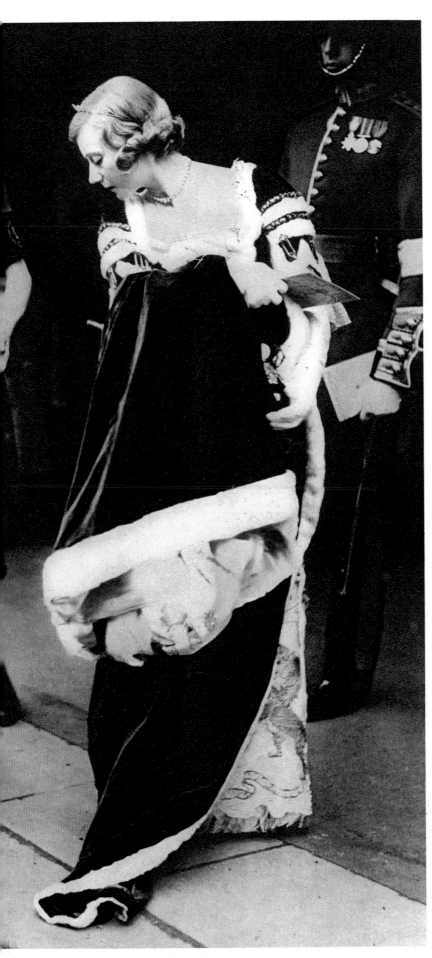

The Earl and Countess of Suffolk at the Annexe.
Lady Suffolk was Miss Mimi Crawford, actress.

LORD AND LADY GREENWOOD

H.H. THE PRINCE AGA KHAN AND THE BEGUM AGA KHAN

THE DUKE AND DUCHESS OF KENT
The Duchess wearing magnificent robes and jewels.
They were leaving their home for the Palace.

Her Majesty the Queen

PRINCESS ELIZABETH MANAGES HER TRAIN

She was received at the Abbey by Earl Marshal the Duke of Norfolk. Standing behind, with her coronet, is Lord Lascelles, the Princess Royal's elder son.

THE REGALIA

Borne in procession by clergy to the High Altar before the service.

THE RECOGNITION:

The King faces to the North, the South, the East, the West as the Primate calls for his Recognition. The answer is the cry "God Save the King."

THE SWORD OF STATE

Delivered to the King. Later it was
carried unsheathed before him.

A RIGHT-HAND GLOVE

Traditional Coronation gift of the Lords of the
Manor of Worksop.

HIS TWO SCEPTRES

The King, wearing the glove presented by the Lords of the Manor of Worksop,
receives the Sceptre with the Cross and the Sceptre with the Dove.

THE KING IS CROWNED

The Primate of All England raises the Crown of St. Edward on high before placing it on the King's head. A moment later the Abbey echoed with the cry : "God Save the King". Drums rolled, silver trumpets sounded and the guns of the Tower boomed in salute.

The Queen sees her Husband Crowned

Sitting in her Chair of Estate, the Queen, her magnificent train spreading round her, watches the Coronation of her husband. Pages stand in a row behind King Edward's Chair. Kings of Arms, Pursuivants are beside the pillars.

HOMAGE

The Duke of Norfolk, representing all of his rank in the peerage, was swearing
fealty to the King after the crowning.   A page holds his coronet.

SWEARING FEALTY

A representative duke, marquis, earl, viscount and baron did
homage to the King, in turn, after his inthronization.

PRIMATE KNEELS AT THE KING'S KNEES

He was the first to do homage ; kissed the King's
left cheek. All the Bishops knelt.

ROBED AND CROWNED

The King invested with the Imperial
Mantle of Cloth of Gold.

The King and Queen,

Crowned, take their Thrones

THE QUEEN IS CROWNED

HOMAGE

H.R.H. The Duke of Gloucester salutes the King at the moment of Crowning, by wearing his coronet.   Peers behind, follow suit, a mass of ermine and shining gold.

THE KING'S PROCESSION

THE QUEEN'S PROCESSION

The Queen with her six trainbearers

King George VI leaves the Abbey

133

THE QUEEN MOTHER'S PROCESSION

Her three grandchildren escort her—Princess Elizabeth, Princess Margaret Rose, Lord Lascelles (holding the train, left). The assembly rise to salute her.

QUEEN MARY LEAVES

Her blue and gold train supported, she moves from the
crowning theatre, down the long nave.

PRIME MINISTERS IN THE ABBEY

Mr. Stanley Baldwin, Prime Minister of Great Britain, with Mr. Ramsay MacDonald,
Lord President of the Council, is followed by Prime Ministers Mackenzie King
(Canada), Lyons (Australia), Savage (New Zealand) and Hertzog (South Africa).

"Sir, is Your Majesty willing to take The Oath?"

The great ceremony in Westminster Abbey begins. The Archbishop of Canterbury, facing the King, asks the preliminary questions before administering the Oath. The King and Queen are seated in their Chairs of Estate. The Coronation Chair is in the middle of the sanctuary; the two thrones are behind it. Seated in their robes, to the right of the thrones, are the Duke of Gloucester, the Duke of Kent and Prince Arthur of Connaught.

TWO CROWNS, TWO SCEPTRES

A good close-up of the King

137

THE GOLDEN COACH LEAVES THE ABBEY

ACCLAIMED BY THOUSANDS AT WESTMINSTER

Recrossing Trafalgar Square: The

procession passes Nelson's Column

Piccadilly Circus

The mounties ride through, watched through a sea of periscopes.
In a bird's eye view from the roof they seem like toy soldiers.

THE GUARDS IN OXFORD STREET

THE PRINCESSES GO BY

Returning from the Abbey

Entering Hyde Park

Through the Sovereign's Gate, Marble Arch

Beneath the Quadriga

Back to the Palace

AND STILL THEY CHEERED

Thousands cheered the King and Queen when they appeared on the balcony of
Buckingham Palace less than half an hour after their return from the Abbey.

MOTHER AND DAUGHTER

The Queen, arm affectionately around her daughter, acknowledges the cheers.

On the Palace Balcony

Queen Mary joined her son and daughter-in-law on the Balcony of Buckingham Palace after their return from the Abbey and received a moving demonstration of affection from the thousands below.

INDIAN HEROES
Troops of many regiments, their uniforms and head-dresses a fascinating blaze of colour, take a "spell" on the steps of the Victoria Memorial.

A CURB-EDGE VIEW
Even the Indian warriors found the long wait exhausting. A contrast in head wear.

TIRED OUT

After eight hours, pages and a peeress rest on the carpeted steps of the annexe.

PEERS SEEK THEIR CARS, PASSING THROUGH CROWDS

Coro

ation Floodlighting Westminster Abbey, Trafalgar Square, and the destroyers Eclipse and Echo outlined in the Thames, off Erith Pier.

LONDON GRANDSTAND
They climbed the Victoria Memorial, near the Palace, on Coronation Night.
Wouldn't come down. So the policeman went up.

The King's Radio Vow

MAY 12th, 1937

Their Coronation Night: The King and Queen appeared for fourth time on balcony; acknowledged cheers of crowd below in rain.

———————— ✳ ————————

"IT is with a very full heart that I speak to you to-night. Never before has a newly-crowned king been able to talk to all his peoples in their own homes on the day of his coronation.

"Never has the ceremony itself had so wide a significance; for the Dominions are now free and equal partners with this ancient kingdom, and I felt this morning that the whole Empire was in very truth gathered within the walls of Westminster Abbey.

"I rejoice that I can now speak to you all, wherever you may be, greeting old friends in distant lands, and, as I hope, new friends in those parts where it has not yet been my good fortune to go.

"In this personal way the Queen and I wish health and happiness to you all; and we do not forget at this time of celebration those who are living under the shadow of sickness or distress.

"Their example of courage and good citizenship is always before us, and to them I would send a special message of sympathy and good cheer.

"I cannot find words with which to thank you for your love and loyalty to the Queen and myself.

"Your good will in the streets to-day, your countless messages from overseas and from every quarter of these islands, have filled our hearts to overflowing.

"I will only say this: If, in the coming years, I can show my gratitude in service to you, that is the way above all others that I should choose.

"To many millions the Crown is the symbol of unity. By the grace of God and by the will of the free peoples of the British Commonwealth, I have assumed that Crown.

"In me, as your King, is vested for a time the duty of maintaining its honour and integrity.

"This is, indeed, a grave and constant responsibility, but it gave me confidence to see your representatives around me in the Abbey and to know that you, too, were enabled to join in that infinitely beautiful ceremonial.

"Its outward forms come down from distant times, but its inner meaning and message are always new, for the highest of distinctions is the service of others, and to the ministry of Kingship I have, in your hearing, dedicated myself, with the Queen at my side, in words of the deepest solemnity.

"We will, God helping us, faithfully discharge our trust.

"Those of you who are children now will, I hope, retain memories of a day of carefree happiness such as I still have of the day of my grandfather's Coronation.

"Some of you in the coming years will travel from one part of the Commonwealth to another, and moving thus within the family circle will meet others whose thoughts are coloured by the same memories, whose hearts unite in devotion to our common heritage.

"You will learn, I hope, how much our free association means to us; how much our friendship with each other, and with all the nations upon earth, can help the cause of peace and progress.

"The Queen and I will always keep in our hearts the inspiration of this day.

"May we ever be worthy of the good will which, I am proud to think, surrounds us at the outset of my reign.

"I thank you from my heart, and may God bless you all."

OFFICIAL CORONATION GROUP

The Royal Family pose in full robes and crowns, in Buckingham Palace. *Left to right :* H.R.H. Princess Royal, H.R.H. Duchess of Gloucester, H.R.H. Duke of Gloucester, Her Majesty Queen Mary, His Majesty King George, Her Majesty Queen Elizabeth, H.R.H. Duke of Kent, H.R.H. Duchess of Kent, Her Majesty The Queen of Norway. *In front :* H.R.H. Princess Margaret Rose, H.R.H. Princess Elizabeth.

"THE Coronation of the King and Queen took place in the Abbey Church of Westminster this day" was the terse way in which the Court Circular summed up at night the tremendous events of May the twelfth.

The eyes of not only millions of his subjects but the ears of the whole world lent themselves to this Coronation of the young King and Queen of the oldest of democracies.

Those who saw their Sovereign in his procession through the streets of London testify to the vision of a man dignified and simple in gesture ; those who watched the actual Crowning gazed down on a king acting with assurance his part in the sacred pageant ; and those who heard his voice on the wireless that night heard a voice they knew and had loved—the firm voice of George the Fifth—the same in intonation and miraculously the same in character.

A burst of sunshine as the Royal Coach left the Palace, the booming crash of cannon when the Crown was placed upon his head, the pealing of the Abbey's bells as the King and Queen left—these were trappings for the splendid pageant of Empire which moved through the streets that day.

Proud dragoons and marching sailors, hussars and turbaned lancers in splendid array ; admirals on horseback and fighting Sikhs on foot ; Canadian Mounted Police behind prime ministers in gilded carriages processed ahead of the warm-golden Coach drawn by its grey horses. Highland pipers, bands on foot and bands mounted, soldiers and princes from all over the world helped in the making of as colourful a page of history as these little islands have ever seen.

That night the King and Queen answered the acclaim of their subjects by four times appearing on the balcony of their floodlit Palace, while the great crowd of nearly 100,000 people stood in the drizzling darkness chanting the National Anthem.

And from Vancouver in the north-west to Tasmania in the south-east ; from Hong-Kong to Bermuda and back again by Cape Town to Trinidad ; from Melbourne to Quebec and from the Orkneys to Auckland came the answering echo of four hundred millions "GOD SAVE THE KING!"

PRINTED BY CLARKE & SHERWELL LTD., LONDON AND NORTHAMPTON

SCOTTISH LINKS

WITH THE

ROYAL FAMILY

by

John Herries McCulloch

A Scottish King For England

CHAPTER ONE

JAMES VI of Scotland was dubbed "The wisest fool in Christendom," and he has been the punching-bag of a great many historians, but in his determination to succeed Queen Elizabeth of England, and the accomplishment of that great desire, he really proved himself to be a practical statesman, for he brought about the Union of the Crowns and paved the way to the Union of the English and Scottish Parliaments.

He became, in fact, the true heir to the English Crown after the execution of his mother, Mary Queen of Scots, in 1587. Nevertheless, Elizabeth would not designate him as her successor. The Pope and the Catholic Kings of France and Spain, were all anxious to keep the Scottish King from succeeding Elizabeth, because he was a Protestant. Their idea was to make England a Catholic country again. Philip, the King of Spain, was toying with the idea of doing it by conquering England. He actually tried it in 1588, with the Armada, but the expedition was a disastrous failure.

Religious questions in Scotland

James was crafty enough to size the situation up, and he became a practical politician, preaching learnedly about the Divine Right of Kings, and making the Catholics believe that he was a very lukewarm Protestant—which he was. He was really an Episcopalian, as he proved during his reign in England. His Catholic nobles tried to bring Spanish soldiers to Scotland, failed, then started a rebellion on their own. James put it down, and the Presbyterian ministers badgered him to wreak his vengeance on the Earl of Huntly and the Earl of Errol. James steered a middle course, with his eye still on England. His stern struggle with the Presbyterians continued, but he agreed to an Act in 1592, which declared that the Church should be Presbyterian, and not Episcopalian. The ministers were elated, but James got around their Magna Charta of 1592 by summoning meetings of the General Assembly and letting the Ministers harangue themselves into quarrels and divisions. James became the master of the Kirk again, and in 1600 actually appointed three bishops. It was the thin edge of the Episcopalian wedge, and James hammered it home before his quarrel with the ministers came to an end. He used the nobles in his struggle, but he was too long-headed to trust them.

JAMES VI OF SCOTLAND, JAMES I OF ENGLAND

He had his kingdom pretty well in hand, and the kirk pretty well subdued, at the turn of the century, and he had left no useful letter unwritten in his efforts to make good his claim to the throne of England. He had Cecil, the real master of England, working secretly for him, and it was the great Elizabethan Secretary who got the expiring Queen to name James as her successor. So, on the night of March 24th, 1603, when the opportunist Sir Robert Carey rode up to Holyrood Palace on a jaded horse with the news that the English Queen was dead, James was prepared to take the road South. He heard Carey's news, but long-headed as ever, waited for a day or two till the news came to him officially. He knew then that he was King of Scotland, England, and Ireland, at the age of thirty-eight.

With the power of England behind him, James governed Scotland "through the post." He chose the members of the Privy Council himself, and they grovelled to him. Years later, when he was battling with the obstinate English Parliament, he declared petulantly : "Here I sit and govern Scotland with my pen ; I write, and it is done ; and by a Clerk of the Council I govern Scotland now, which others could not do by the sword."

Commissioners to treat of a Union with the English Commissioners was Patrick, 9th Lord Glamis, who was one of James's Privy Councillors. James was defeated in his efforts by the unpopularity of Scotsmen who were then living in England. That may seem like a loose statement, made for picturesque purposes, but it is a hard fact, and while it would be idle to say that other factors did not help to make impotent the negotiations for the Union of the Parliaments of England and Scotland, race hatred put an end to the discussions. James's attitude throughout was commendable in every way, and it was certainly no fault of his that the great project of Parliamentary Union was not achieved until a century later.

Scots in London

Volumes could be written about the Scottish people who followed their king to London. Some of them were mendacious sycophants. Others were downright blackguards. Others, again, were decent folk who were looking for chances to find work and better themselves. Many of the last-mentioned classification became important figures in London. George Heriot, the Edinburgh goldsmith, who really acted as banker for King James and Queen Anne as well, was a tower of probity and business sagacity. David Ramsay, a Dalkeith man, established himself as a watchmaker in London, but the records show that he was an inventive genius, with many useful patents to his name. Indeed, he was one of England's very first registered inventors, and certainly the greatest of his period.

THE ELECTOR PALATINE FREDERICK V

It was too true. The Scottish Parliament had lost any authority it ever had, the Privy Council was composed of men who lived in terror of doing something, even with good intentions, that would offend James, and he kept them busy with his Royal Letters. Scotland was governed by these Royal Letters. No sensible person would argue that this system of government was good for Scotland, or that it was even sound in theory, but in view of James's experiences as a ruler in his ancient Kingdom, what other course could be expected of him? The Scottish people had never shown unity, or the desire to be reasonable; on the other hand, when it came to the bit, they wilted completely when the new King of England breathed the slightest displeasure upon them.

PRINCESS ELIZABETH, DAUGHTER OF JAMES I

Married the Elector Palatine Frederick V. Subsequently they became King and Queen of Bohemia. Elizabeth's children included the great Prince Rupert and Sophia who married the Elector of Hanover, and became the mother of George I of England.

Scottish generosity

That these prominent men were surrounded by a colony of industrious, respectable, and kind-hearted Scots in London is proven by the establishment of the Scots Poor Box in 1613. A group of Scottish journeymen brought it into existence by pledging themselves to help each other. The entrance fee to this curious friendly society was five shillings, and each member put in sixpence every three months. The accumulated money was loaned out to needy members of the group without interest, or spent to meet the expenses of sickness and burial. The Society was granted a Charter in 1665, under the title of the Scottish Corporation, and it still exists, in the form of a rich and carefully-managed trust.

James really destroyed the sovereignty of Scotland. He did not even pay his ancient and subservient kingdom the courtesy of a visit until he had been in England eighteen years, but he had no enmity towards his native country and took a practical and indeed spacious view of its political future. With this view before his mind's eye, he tried hard to bring about the complete political union of the two countries, and it is a curious fact that one of the Scots

While the Scots Poor Box was being established, however,

**ROBERT CECIL
FIRST EARL OF SALISBURY**
"The real master of England . . . worked secretly for James"

King James and his new subjects were being pestered and angered by another type of Scot in London. These disturbers of England's peace were mostly debt-collectors and penniless ruffians. The debt collectors bothered the king—for he had left a lot of unpaid bills in Edinburgh—and the penniless ruffians annoyed the English. So objectionable were the immigrants from Scotland, in fact, that a succession of severely-worded Proclamations were issued for the purpose of getting rid of them. Here is one of them :

"THAT IN CONSIDERATION OF THE RESORT OF IDLE PERSONS OF LOW CONDITION FORTH FROM HIS MAJESTY'S KINGDOM OF SCOTLAND, TO HIS ENGLISH COURT, FILLING THE SAME WITH THEIR SUITS AND SUPPLICATIONS AND DISHONOURING THE ROYAL PRESENCE WITH THEIR BASE, POOR, AND BEGGARLY PERSONS, TO THE DISGRACE OF THEIR COUNTRY IN THE ESTIMATION OF THE ENGLISH ; THESE ARE TO PROHIBIT THE SKIPPERS, MASTERS OF VESSELS, AND OTHERS, IN EVERY PART OF SCOTLAND, FROM BRINGING SUCH MISERABLE CREATURES UP TO COURT, UNDER PAIN OF FINE AND IMPRISONMENT."

England v. Scotland

The animosity shown by the English at this time towards the Scots who were flocking towards London, reached its greatest intensity during the Parliamentary debates on the subject of the Union of the English and Scottish Parliaments. Some of the denunciations of the Scottish race heard on the floor of the House were so violent, in fact, that King James had to intervene. Sir Christopher Piggott, for instance, stated that there were "Well-deserving Scots," but, he continued, "Were not many of the Scots murderers, thieves, and rogues, and was there not one damning peculiarity in Scottish history generally ? They had not suffered above two kings to die in their beds these two hundred years ; our king hath hardly escaped them ; they have attempted him ; why let them in to repeat their pranks on him and his successors in England ?"

James stepped in, and Sir Christopher had to receive a severe reprimand on his knees, was committed to the Tower, and his seat in Bucks declared vacant.

Nevertheless, Sir Christopher voiced the opinion of most Englishmen about the invading Scots, and it was this opinion, as has been stated already, which really did as much as anything else to bring the Union negotiations to a standstill.

England Re-linked with the Stuarts

CHAPTER TWO

KING JAMES and Queen Anne had several children who died in infancy in Scotland, but the surviving children became notable. They were Henry, a young man of great talent and personal charm, who died of typhoid fever when he was eighteen—the enemies of the king spread the monstrous calumny that the Prince was poisoned by his jealous father—Elizabeth and Charles. The reckless and unhappy career of Charles, who succeeded his father, may be passed over, but the career of the Princess Elizabeth is of particular interest because it was such an important link in the long chain that stretches from the present Royal Family to the House of Stuart.

The Princess Elizabeth

The fact is seldom mentioned, but Elizabeth was one of the most handsome Princesses that this country has ever produced. There is a good portrait of her in Holyrood Palace, and it alone is sufficient proof of her commanding beauty. She had a good figure, like her mother, had strong but regular features, and her whole expression is one of arresting femininity in the strong modern note. Few portraits of royal women of her period have such an authentic touch ; one sees at once that Elizabeth was a strikingly handsome woman, with a magnetic personality.

A Wedding is arranged

Early in 1612, the Count Palatine was mentioned seriously as her future husband, and the usual negotiations for the match were begun. On October 22nd, the prospective bridegroom arrived in London, saw the Princess, and became a willing party to the marriage contract. For

Elizabeth, it was the opening chapter of a long and dreary story of exile, disillusionment, and sadness, for she was destined to become a martyr to the stupidity of her husband and the dubious cause of Continental Protestantism.

The Lord Mayor of London gave a dinner to the Count Palatine late in October—and it was noticed that the Prince of Wales was absent. He was ill, and died on November 6th, in the midst of the wedding preparations.

The Elector Palatine and Elizabeth were married, but soon afterwards their troubles began. The Protestants of Bohemia, in open rebellion against the Emperor, had offered the Elector the vacant throne of their broken country, and he made the mistake of accepting it, thereby challenging his Emperor. War resulted, and the end of it found the King of Bohemia a refugee in Holland.

Ancestors of George VI

Meanwhile, Elizabeth, his wife, had given birth to Rupert, who became the great Prince Rupert, of military fame, another son who was christened Maurice, and a daughter called Sophia. Sophia married the Elector of Hanover, and George the First was a child of that union. Charles, the son of James the First, started the wrecking process that ended the long line of Stuart kings, but James's daughter Elizabeth brought the Stuart blood back to the British throne, through the line of the Georges. That line, as the genealogical tree on page 167 shows, produced Queen Victoria, King Edward VII, King George V, King Edward VIII, who abdicated, and the present monarch, George VI.

As Duke of York, King George VI married Lady Elizabeth Bowes-Lyon, daughter of the Earl of Strathmore, of Glamis Castle, Forfarshire, and their first-born child, born April 21st, 1926, was christened Elizabeth. This charming little Princess is therefore heir-presumptive to the British throne, and it is a curious fact that she bears the same name as the Princess who brought the blood of the Royal Stuarts back to the throne of this country.

Two Nations at Loggerheads

CHAPTER THREE

SCOLDING the English Parliament on May 2nd, 1607, because it was moving too slowly in the matter of a Parliamentary Union of his two kingdoms, King James

THE PARENTS OF JAMES I OF ENGLAND
Unhappy Mary, Queen of Scots, and Lord Darnley

exclaimed angrily: "I protest to God, the fruits thereof will chiefly tend to your own weal, prosperity, and increasing greatness."

The proposed Union, he declared, "is an eternal agreement and reconciliation of many long, bloody wars."

It was all true, and yet, in spite of James's best efforts to bring the two countries into one political body, the negotiations fell through. The people of England did not want a union of the two Parliaments. Neither did the people of Scotland. If King James had been younger, he would undoubtedly have pushed his great scheme through, for he was extremely tenacious and dexterous in promoting his own ideas of good government. He was past his prime, however, and already suffering from a variety of painful ailments, and he had so many other serious problems of statecraft to face, at home and abroad, that he was obliged to drop the project that was so close to his heart.

Parliamentary Union again

After his death, England became involved in the costly quarrels abroad which he had always preached against, crowned heads fell, revolution reared its head, and there was no more talk of a complete Parliamentary Union with Scotland until the reign of Queen Anne.

Anne was keen for the Union, advocating it strongly in her first speech to the English Parliament, and the negotiations which had been started by King James nearly a century previously were in due course resumed — but they were resumed under very curious circumstances.

Scottish Parliament

At that time, the beginning of the eighteenth century, the Scottish Parliament consisted of members elected by the Three Estates. There were thirty-five nobles, thirty-eight Commissioners of the Shires, and forty-three Commissioners of the Burghs, but although the nobles were in the minority, they had no difficulty in dominating the other two Estates. This was owing to their influence as landowners, their capacity for public work, and the traditional attitude of humility which Scotsmen adopted towards men bearing exalted titles. The clergy had been shut out at the time of the Revolution, but they were a powerful and very active party in the country.

It is interesting to look back at the last Scottish Parliament that sat in Edinburgh. It was in no sense a democratic

AT BALMORAL
Queen Mary with King George VI and Queen Elizabeth (then Duke and Duchess of York)

Anne pressed for a complete political union of the two countries, was a merry-go-round, run by the nobles to the strident music of Whiggery and Presbyterianism. We shall see how this moribund assembly approached the great project of Parliamentary Union.

Immediately after Anne's accession in 1702, the English Parliament passed an Act to make it obligatory for all persons holding office to abjure her brother, the Pretender. A glance at the foregoing genealogical tree will show why the English were anxious to cut off the Stuart claimants to the throne. The extreme Presbyterians of Scotland were demanding that an Act with the same object be passed by the Scottish Parliament.

At that time, the Lord Chancellor and President of the House in Scotland was the Earl of Marchmont, a very astute man. He brought in a bill for abjuring the Prince of Wales, which of course meant that no Catholic would thenceforth be Scotland's king.

The bill split the House in two, 57 voting for a second reading and 53 voting the opposite way. The Commissioner Queensberry saved the situation by proroguing the House till August. When the Scottish Estates declined to pass this Act of Abjuration, they were, of course, thumbing their noses at England. Realizing that they had been pretty defiant, they made amends to some extent by passing the Act of Union.

The meeting of Commissioners

At Anne's suggestion, the English Parliament had already passed a bill ordaining that Commissioners of the Union should be chosen from both countries, and Queensberry, the Scottish Commissioner—who really took his orders from the English Secretary of State—was expected to get a similar bill put through the Scottish Parliament. He got the bill put through, and Queen Anne was therefore in a position to appoint Commissioners from both Kingdoms.

Queensberry hurried down to London to report what he had done, and in due course the Commission for Union met—on November 10th, 1702. There were 23 English Commissioners and 22 from Scotland, and their first meeting was held in the Cockpit at Whitehall.

Even at that time, the English Commissioners were not a bit keen about the projected Union. So indifferent were they that they began to stay away from the meetings of the Commission; on eight occasions, in fact, so many of them were absent that a quorum could not be made. However, it was agreed that there should be a common legislature, and that the succession

body. The nobles took their places in it because they held Crown Lands. The Commissioners for the Shires were elected by Crown vassals who could show that they held lands to the value of forty shillings. Each of the sixty-six Royal Burghs in the country was entitled to send one representative to Parliament, but the voting was done by the town councils. Worse still, the town councils of that day had developed the ancient French habit of electing their successors, so that elections to Parliament were an endless game of wire-pulling, in which the public had small part indeed.

Corruption

Actually, the Privy Council controlled the Parliamentary elections, and suitable members were secured for Edinburgh by a widespread system of petty graft and corruption. The votes of Freeholders were bought by the distribution of pensions and small offices, and the bigger fish were landed by dangling the bait of higher titles or important offices of State in front of them.

The Parliamentary scene in Scotland, therefore, at the time when Queen

Table showing how Queen Elizabeth of Bohemia linked the House of Stuart with the present Royal Family

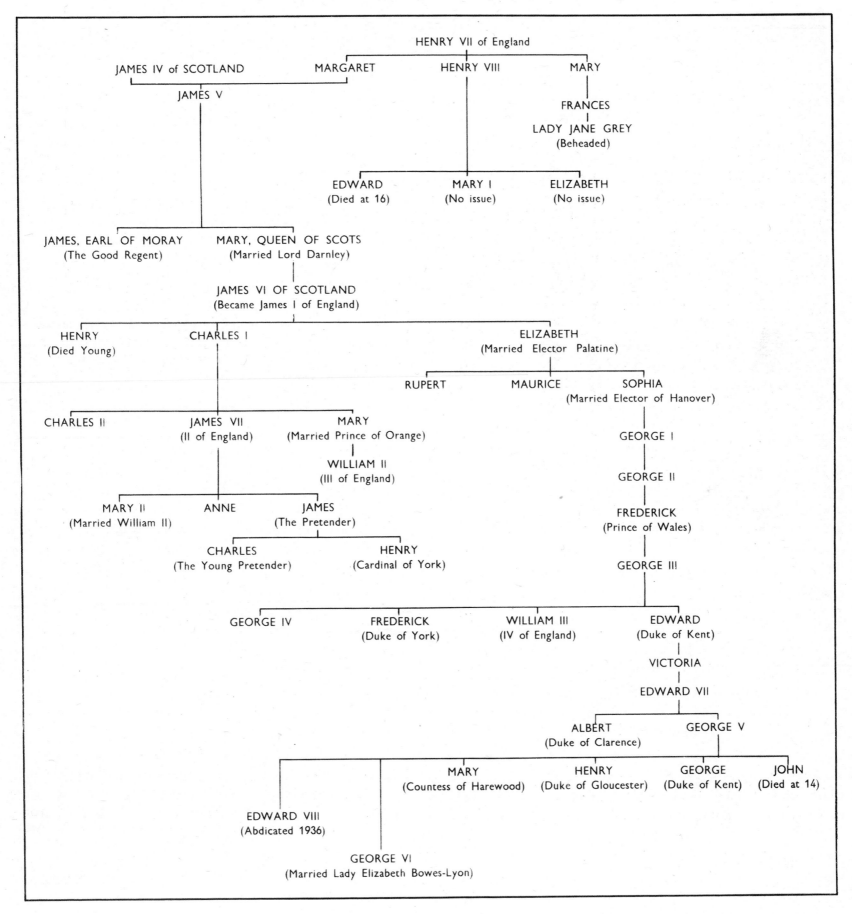

HENRY VII of England

JAMES IV of SCOTLAND — MARGARET — HENRY VIII — MARY

JAMES V

FRANCES

LADY JANE GREY
(Beheaded)

EDWARD
(Died at 16)

MARY I
(No issue)

ELIZABETH
(No issue)

JAMES, EARL OF MORAY
(The Good Regent)

MARY, QUEEN OF SCOTS
(Married Lord Darnley)

JAMES VI OF SCOTLAND
(Became James I of England)

HENRY
(Died Young)

CHARLES I

ELIZABETH
(Married Elector Palatine)

RUPERT — MAURICE — SOPHIA
(Married Elector of Hanover)

CHARLES II

JAMES VII
(II of England)

MARY
(Married Prince of Orange)

GEORGE I

WILLIAM II
(III of England)

GEORGE II

MARY II
(Married William II)

ANNE

JAMES
(The Pretender)

FREDERICK
(Prince of Wales)

CHARLES
(The Young Pretender)

HENRY
(Cardinal of York)

GEORGE III

GEORGE IV

FREDERICK
(Duke of York)

WILLIAM III
(IV of England)

EDWARD
(Duke of Kent)

VICTORIA

EDWARD VII

ALBERT
(Duke of Clarence)

GEORGE V

MARY
(Countess of Harewood)

HENRY
(Duke of Gloucester)

GEORGE
(Duke of Kent)

JOHN
(Died at 14)

EDWARD VIII
(Abdicated 1936)

GEORGE VI
(Married Lady Elizabeth Bowes-Lyon)

should descend on the Electress Sophia and her heirs. Sophia, as the foregoing genealogical table shows, was the daughter of Elizabeth, and a granddaughter of King James the First of England, so that the line of the Pretender had been cut out, although the blood of the Stuarts had been infused back into our royal line. Having done that much, the Commission rose on February 3rd, 1703, with the intention of meeting again in the following October, but it had become so weak that it never met again.

Decline of Scottish Government

Meanwhile, the Scottish Commissioner Queensberry continued to take his orders from England, which shows how the lack of a King had weakened Scotland politically.

The Union of Parliaments
CHAPTER FOUR

THE new Parliament met on May 6th, 1703, and after two years of squabbling passed the Act of Security, by way of replying to England's Act of Settlement, passed two years previously. It is necessary, in order to understand the peculiar history of the Union of Parliaments, to know the exact meanings of these two Acts.

In 1701, a year before Anne ascended the throne, the English Parliament passed the Act of Settlement, which declared that on the death of Anne, the crown should go to Sophia, Electress of Hanover. That meant that Sophia

THE QUEEN'S PARENTS

The 14th Earl of Strathmore and Kinghorne

THE EARL'S COAT OF ARMS
The Motto reads: "In Thee, O Lord, have I put my trust"

The Countess of Strathmore and Kinghorne

The English statesmen wanted a new Parliament in Scotland, but Queensberry advised against an election. The real manager of Scotland, the Earl of Nottingham, England's Secretary of State, did not accept Queensberry's advice, and the latter was such a tool of the English statesmen that the Scottish Parliament was dissolved and a new one elected at the end of that year. Nothing could more clearly show how much Scotland was governed by England at that time.

The election caused a first-class political row in Scotland, as the Kirk was opposed to it. It was carried through, however, by the Earl of Seafield, a smooth, able, and cold-blooded Scottish politician who was highly valued by Queen Anne and her ministers. Seafield had been appointed joint Secretary of State with Queensberry at the time of Anne's accession, and although he was one of these oily politicians who seem to have no friends except in high places, he put the election across, by making threats here and there, by distributing pensions, and offices, and by promising his supporters future rewards. Considering how the voting was done in Scotland at that time, Seafield's system was almost bound to be successful.

would become Scotland's queen as well, yet the Scottish people had never been consulted about the Act.

Independence

They were insulted by such rough-shod treatment, and the new Scottish Parliament showed this by passing the Act of Security, which stated that a successor to Anne was to be chosen twenty days after she died, if she died without issue. Moreover, the Act declared that this successor must be a Protestant, and a descendant of the House of Stuart, but he or she could not be chosen by the English unless they agreed that Scotland should have free religion, free government, and free trade.

Here was a fine kettle of fish! The Scottish Act simply meant that after Anne's death Scotland might take it into her head to select a different sovereign from England, and so become a separate nation once more. England became alarmed, and angry as well. She hit back with "An Act for the effectual Securing the Kingdom of England from the apparent dangers that may arise from several Acts lately passed in the Parliament of Scotland."

The Act had real teeth in it, for it stated that "should no treaty be effected by December 25th, 1705, all Scotsmen,

NEW COLOURS FOR THE BLACK WATCH

The Duke and Duchess of York at Glamis Castle, August 1935, where the Duchess presented Colours to the 4/5 Battalion, Black Watch.

THE BRAEMAR GATHERING, 1934

The Duchess of York, wearing a hunting Stuart tartan kilt, is greeted on her arrival. Queen Mary and the Princesses have moved towards the Royal Pavilion.

except such as were settled in England, would be treated as aliens ; no horses, arms, or ammunition would be supplied to Scotland from England ; Scottish cattle, linens, and coals would be excluded both from England and Ireland."

An unpleasant incident

To such a sorry pass had things come between England and Scotland, less than two years before they became fully united. The sober truth is that they were bitter enemies, and ready to go to war with each other. England was actually concerned about strengthening her northern fortresses ; Scotland had made provision for an army of her own. The intensity of the common enmity at this time was shown by the horrible affair of the Worcester. In 1705 a ship belonging to the Scottish African Company had been seized in the Thames, at the behest of the hated East India Company. The English authorities ignored the protests of the Scottish Company, so when an English ship called the Worcester came into Leith, the Secretary of the Scottish African Company took the law into his own hands and boarded the ship with an armed mob at his back and took Captain Green and his crew off as prisoners.

So strong was the feeling of hatred against England that the mobs of Edinburgh howled for the execution of the English Captain and his crew, on the trumped-up charge that the Worcester had been mixed up with piracy. Queen Anne sent documentary proof to Seafield, her creature in Scotland, of the innocence of Captain Green and his men, but although Chancellor Seafield and the other Scottish Ministers had this proof in their possession, they were in such terror of the mobs that they allowed the English skipper and two members of his crew to be executed on the Links of Leith.

The Climax

It was the ugliness of the feeling between the two countries that really brought about the Union of Parliaments. They had come so close to war that to avoid war the statesmen of both countries got together hurriedly and rushed through the Treaty of Union. The story of the subsequent negotiations and manipulations is a long one, and not very pleasant reading for Scotsmen. George Baillie of Jerviswoode, who was one of the most able supporters of the Union, said of the Scottish people ; "Considering the temper of this people, how unfit to govern themselves !"

Considering the prejudices, hatreds, schisms, and base treacheries that racked and degraded Scotland at that time, Baillie had good reason for making that remark. Indeed, the country was probably saved from itself by the men who

**HON. LL.D.
OF ST. ANDREW'S**

at opening of new graduation hall, 1929

were leading it into the Union, for while some of them were unscrupulous self-seekers, and others were no more than the fawning political valets of the English Secretary of State, they at least had intelligence and foresight, and were big enough to work together for the good of their country. The two Commissions met on April 16th, 1706, at Whitehall, and they were so afraid that the people of Scotland would conclude that their representatives were being subdued by English blandishments that there was no interchange of hospitality whatever during the whole course of the negotiations.

England and Scotland United

So, at the second meeting of the two Commissions, it was mutually agreed, among other things, that :

1. The two Kingdoms should be united under the name of Great Britain.

2. The United Kingdom should be represented by one Parliament, Scotland sending 16 peers to the House of Lords and 45 members to the House of Commons.

3. The Succession to the crown should devolve on the House of Hanover, in accordance with the English Act of Settlement.

4. That both countries were to have one flag, on which the Cross of St. Andrew, Scotland's patron saint, and the Cross of St. George, England's patron saint, were to be placed.

5. Both Countries were to be subject to the same system of taxation, and that they were to have equal trading rights, with the same coinage, weights and measures.

6. The laws and Law Courts of both countries were to remain as they were.

It remained to secure the acceptance of the Treaty by both Parliaments. In the English Parliament it met with no opposition, but it had a stormy passage through the last Scottish Parliament, which met on October 3rd, 1706. For three months the members argued, and blood was nearly spilled on the floor of the House. Savage riots broke out in Edinburgh, Glasgow, and Dumfries. The Duke of Queensberry, Scotland's Lord High Commissioner, was stoned as he drove to Parliament. The enraged mobs even tried to invade Parliament House. At last, in fear and trembling, the Parliament passed the Treaty, and on January 16th, 1707, the Commissioner touched it with the royal Sceptre to signify that it had become law.

England and Scotland had become one country.

WELCOMED TO THE WESTERN ISLES
The King and Queen arriving in the storied Island of Skye

The Dark Days Following the Union

CHAPTER FIVE

SCOTLAND, as we have seen, had given up her monarchy, then her Parliament, but statesmen in both countries felt confident or pretended to feel confident, that her sacrifices would be amply justified by the value of her new political association.

So far as Scotland was concerned, these happy predictions were not justified for a long time to come. Theoretically, Scotland shared England's wealth at home and abroad, but that did not do very much towards increasing prosperity in Scotland. On the other hand, Scotland was faced with the necessity of joining England in any war in which she became involved, and supplying her quota of the sinews of war. At the time of the Union, indeed, England was at war with France, so that Scotland found herself in the odious position of being at war with her ancient ally of the continent. Scotland's trade with France had always been profitable, but now it was cut off, with serious loss.

Loss of Trade—Heavier Taxation

It was inevitable, also, in view of the rising taxation in England, that the bad results of the Union would be felt first in Scotland. England was imposing high duties on a large number of articles imported from foreign countries, and Scotland had now to pay these duties. The result of this was that Scotland's trade with foreign countries was crippled to some extent, and this, in turn, created unemployment and poverty in the industrial centres of the country.

On top of all that came heavier taxes, to meet England's budget, and—almost as bad as the taxes themselves—a rigid and efficient system of collection that brought Englishmen into Scotland as tax-collectors.

More cause for dissatisfaction

There was, too, the aggravating matter of "The Equivalent," that thinly-disguised bribe which England offered to Scotland as part of the Treaty of Union, under the pretext of encouraging Scotland's trade and making up for the terrible losses suffered by so many Scottish people in the failure of the Darien Expedition. The Darien Expedition, which had been planned from the first by William Patterson, the Dumfries-shire man who founded the Bank of England, was brought to grief largely by the malign opposition of the English Government, which explains why it was mentioned in connection with "The Equivalent."

The money, amounting to £400,000, was supposed to be handed over as soon as the Union became a reality, but it was slow in coming north, and when it did arrive, drawn by twelve waggons and guarded by more than a hundred soldiers, an Edinburgh mob stoned the English dragoons. Even after that, "The Equivalent" caused great dissatisfaction, for the cash was distributed among a comparatively small number of people, and even among those who did get a share of it—some had to be content with as little as £11—there was dissatisfaction and resentment.

The bald truth is that the Union had done nothing for Scotland, and a vast majority of the people really believed that it had ruined the country. The ministers of the kirk, always a potent force in shaping public opinion, were growling against Union because it had restored patronage, by taking away from the congregations the right of choosing their ministers. The nobles were denouncing it because they were not receiving the privileges they had expected as peers in the House of Lords.

In fact, just before Queen Anne died, in 1714, it looked as if the Union would be broken. England and Scotland were on most unfriendly terms, Scotland, as we have seen, had gained nothing by sacrificing so much, and even some of the Scottish statesmen who had worked hard to bring about the Union were now frankly dubious about it. So strong was the feeling, in both countries, that the Union had been a mistake, that it was proposed in the House of Lords that each country should go back to the old basis. The feeling about it in both countries was shown by the fact that this proposal almost carried, for it was defeated by a mere four votes.

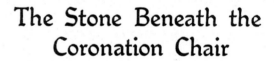

Glamis Castle

Turn of the Tide

The Union held, however, and at long last, after weathering the disastrous upheavals of the 'Fifteen Rebellion, the Affair of the Porteous Mob (1736), and the 'Forty-five Rebellion, the tide of prosperity turned and began to flow towards distressed Scotland. After those forty years of hard and unruly times, it could scarcely be argued that the Union produced the bettered times that did come at the middle of the eighteenth century, but come they did, and Union began to get less blame and more praise.

The prosperity came, as a matter of fact, as a result of the improvement of manufacturing processes in Scotland and the introduction of new ones. The manufacture of linen was the best example of this improvement in industry, and it brought wealth to Scotland, as we know, and laid the foundations of our marvellously efficient and sound banking system.

Then, too, Scotsmen became very active in the trade with the American Colonies, with which, before the Union, they had not been permitted to do business. The cities along the Clyde reaped the harvest of this new trade, exporting linen to the Colonies and bringing back cargoes of tobacco. Great fortunes were built up in this highly

profitable trade. Glasgow, Greenock, and Paisley became exceedingly prosperous and this prosperity was traceable directly to the terms of the Treaty of Union.

Permanent Friendship Established

Scotland had "come through the reek," and while it is safe to say that she would have won her way back to prosperity if the Union had never gone through, her trade channels had been opened up, and England became an increasingly valuable customer for Scottish manufactured articles and agricultural products as the years passed. There was less and less adverse criticism of the Union, less and less enmity towards England, and by the beginning of the nineteenth century the two countries were well accustomed to the bond uniting them, and the country as a whole was entering the Age of Steam and the great Industrial Era, which was to make the Empire the richest that the world has even seen, governed, in the main, by intellectual giants, in the benign shadow of a firmly-established and enlightened monarchial system which has proven, again and again, its extraordinary potency as a cementing force in the strange conglomeration of races comprising the British Commonwealth of Nations.

In the building of that modern Commonwealth, at home and abroad, Scotland has assuredly done her part, and it is fitting, surely, that our present Queen should be a Scotswoman. Indeed, as we shall see in the following chapter, there is an ancient tradition that the Coronation Chair, towards which the eyes of the Empire are now turning, is the symbol of Scottish sovereignty, and that wherever it may be, there the Scots shall reign.

The Stone Beneath the Coronation Chair

CHAPTER SIX

FIXED beneath the seat of the chair on which King George VI will be crowned this year, is a roughly-hewn block of red sandstone. It is not impressive, but it is at least a thousand years old, and while seated on it the ancient kings of Scotland were crowned. It is the Fatal Stone of Scone, and it is safe to say that it is the oldest coronation symbol in existence.

Its earliest history is lost in the mists of antiquity. Legend has it that the stone was the pillow of Jacob, and that it was carried from the Holy Land to Spain, thence to Ireland. According to Irish legends, it was the sacred stone on which the ancient kings of Ireland were crowned, on the hill of Tarah. From Ireland it was supposed to have passed into Argyllshire, where, at Dunstaffnage, it became a Coronation Chair for Scottish kings.

It is more than probable that these legends are a tissue of folk-lore fiction, but there is no doubt that the stone was used as a Coronation Chair at the very dawn of history in Scotland, or that it has been in continuous use ever since at Coronations in this country.

Kenneth, the son of Alpin, moved the Stone from Argyllshire to Scone, near Perth, in the year 838 A.D., possibly to mark the defeat of the Picts, and from that time until 1296, every Scottish king was crowned while seated on it.

By Kenneth's act of depositing the Stone at Scone, that place was invested with holiness and regality. The most

of Alexander III failed to produce a successor to the Scottish throne. Prior to the death of the King of Norway's daughter—she was the last of Alexander's line—a Convention of the Scottish Estates was held at Scone, for the purpose of settling the matter of the succession. The Convention assented to the marriage of the King of Norway's daughter with the son of Edward I of England, and everything seemed to point to a long period of peace between England and Scotland, as a result of this match, when, alas! the young Princess suddenly died.

Then came dark days for Scotland. Its throne was empty.

LANDING IN SKYE
The King and Queen, as Duke and Duchess of York, at Portree, 1933.

ancient Council of which there is any record in Scottish history was held there in the year 906, during the reign of King Constantine, when he and his advisors "solemnly vowed to observe the laws and discipline of faith, the rights of the churches, and of the Gospel, on a little hill near the Royal City of Scone."

These inaugural stones were very common in both Scotland and Ireland a thousand years ago. Kings sat on them to be crowned, but lesser lights used them for ceremonial purposes. The Chief of a Clan, for instance, was inaugurated on a Fatal Stone, and the stone, ever afterwards, became a treasured heirloom of the family concerned. They were symbols of succession.

Malcolm was crowned on the Stone at Scone in 1055, and its royal function was never endangered until the lineage

There were two claimants for the crown, Baliol and Bruce. The country was divided, and its weakness permitted Edward of England to step into the Scottish scene. He chose to support Baliol—chiefly because Baliol was a weakling—and Bruce, the stronger character, was pushed into the background. Baliol was crowned at Scone, and from that moment became the willing tool of Edward.

The English dictator was so offensive and overbearing that even the complaisant Baliol was obliged to kick over the traces. When he did, he was promptly dethroned and hustled into exile.

Edward the First of England had now become master of Scotland, and he made an end of Coronations on the Fatal Stone at Scone. During his reign of terror in the northern kingdom, he destroyed all the visible symbols of Scotland's

LORD HIGH COMMISSIONER 1929

King George VI, as Duke of York and Lord High Commissioner, with the Duchess.

her puppet, was crowned at Scone on September 27th, 1332.

Scotland was entering the Stuart Period, and she retained her independence, although by a precarious margin. The Royal City of Scone, however, had seen its best days. Robert III was crowned there on August 13th, 1390. So was James I on May 21st, 1424, following his captivity of nineteen years in English prisons. After that, Scone became eclipsed. Edinburgh had become the metropolis of Scotland, and the seat of government. All the Legislative Assemblies were held there. It had become the Capital, and it remained the Capital of the Stuarts until James VI succeeded Queen Elizabeth of England. He fixed the seat of his government in England's capital, and when he did that, he made an end of the great displays which had always been a feature of Scottish royalty and Scottish Coronations.

True, James's successors, being monarchs of two distinct kingdoms, were obliged to receive the crown of each in their respective countries, but the distinction was finally wiped out, as we have already seen, by the Union of Parliaments. Charles II was the last British king to be crowned at Scone. He came from exile to be crowned, but found himself in a hot-bed of religious fanaticism, vulgarity, rudeness, and downright treachery. During his coronation his covenanting friends did nothing but howl prayers and chant tuneless hymns. It was a sorry finale to the long period of royal pageantry at Scone.

The Fatal Stone had remained all this time in England, but there was an old Bardic prophecy which ran :

"Except old Seers do feign,
"And Wizard wits be blind :
"The Scots in place must reign,
"Where they this stone shall find."

Curiously enough, the old prophecy has been borne out to a remarkable extent by history. On the death of Queen Elizabeth, James VI of Scotland became ruler of England, and we have seen that Scottish blood still flows in the veins of our Royal Family. Stranger still, in this year of Our Lord 1937, a Scotswoman of ancient lineage is Queen of Great Britain.

It has been argued that the Coronation ceremonies should be repeated in Edinburgh, but in view of the political evolution of Great Britain, such a repetition cannot be justified except on the grounds of courtesy. Scotland is now part and parcel of Great Britain, of which the acknowledged Capital is London, and to argue, as some zealots do, that British monarchs should be crowned in Scotland, as well as in England, is to ignore the hard realities of history. Scotland gave up her right to a separate coronation when her last Parliament passed the Act of Union, and she has far less right to the ceremony than our self-governing Dominions which, by virtue of the Statute of Westminster, are separate Kingdoms within the Commonwealth.

vaunted independence, in order to humble his new subjects. He banished all the troublesome nobles and destroyed the public records. It was not to be expected that he would miss the Fatal Stone at Scone, and he removed it and had it carried to Westminster. There he had it placed in a new chair—at a cost of £1 : 19 : 7—and the chair was placed near the Altar, before the shrine of St. Edward.

Border Warfare

The red tide of war ebbed and flowed across the Border. Sir William Wallace rose up and struck a blow at the tyrants which echoed throughout Scotland. Treachery, however, brought Wallace to an awful death in London, and Scotland again felt the iron heel until Bruce collected an army and fought his way to Scone. There he was solemnly crowned and inaugurated on March 27th, 1306.

His valour had won Scotland her old independence, and the English acknowledged the fact in the Treaty of Northampton, made in 1328. In that Treaty, moreover, which was duly confirmed by Parliament, it was agreed that the Fatal Stone of Scone should be returned to Scotland. To carry this agreement out, writs were actually issued by Edward III, but they were never executed, for the English ruler had never forgiven Scotland, and only awaited an opportunity to attack her again.

The opportunity came when King Robert of Scotland died. He was succeeded by his son David, who was a minor. With this young weakling on the Scottish throne, England again began to dominate the northern kingdom, and Baliol,

Scotland gives England a Queen

CHAPTER SEVEN

KING GEORGE the Sixth was born at York Cottage, Sandringham, on December 14th, 1895.

Queen Elizabeth was born at St. Paul's, Waldenburg, Hertfordshire, England, on August 4th, 1900.

They met for the first time at a party given by Lady Leicester. The King, then Prince Albert, was a shy and stuttering boy of ten ; Lady Elizabeth Angela Marguerite Bowes-Lyon was a fluffy-haired young lady of five. Prince Albert remembered that she had been eating iced cake with more gusto than care !

Their educational needs and the Great War separated them. Prince Albert entered the Royal Naval Training School at Osborne in 1907, and a year later went on to the Royal Naval College at Dartmouth. In 1912 he visited Canada, while serving in the Royal Navy as a Cadet, and in 1913 he was appointed as Midshipman to H.M.S. Battleship Collingwood. The Great War found him in service as a sailor. In 1914 he took ill at sea—he was never a robust lad—and was moved to Aberdeen, where he was operated on for appendicitis. He rejoined his ship and saw service at the Battle of Jutland, but in 1915 he was again overtaken with an obstinate attack of gastric disorder which interrupted his career at sea.

He was serving in the Royal Air Force when peace was declared in 1918, and afterwards visited the American troops at Coblenz, Germany, and spent some time with the headquarters staff of the Canadian Corps at Bonn, Germany.

Romance

In the meantime, he had met Lady Elizabeth Bowes-Lyon again, and fell in love. In 1920 Prince Albert was created Duke of York, and as Duke of York he wooed the blue-eyed and charming young lady he had met at Lady Leicester's party. In 1923 their engagement was announced, and the whole Empire rejoiced. The romance came to its happy climax in the same year, when Lady Elizabeth became the Duchess of York.

Despite the fact that she was born in England, Queen Elizabeth is of pure Scottish descent. As the daughter of the Earl and Countess of Strathmore, of Glamis Castle, Forfarshire, she belongs to one of the oldest and most distinguished Scottish families. Indeed, she could lay claim

to more than that, for the blood of the old Stewart Kings flows in her veins, and she actually brings another infusion of that potent blood into our Royal Family. It will be interesting to trace this hereditary connection, which takes us right back to Scotland's hero king—the Bruce.

Glamis—pronounced Glams—is one of the very oldest family names in Scotland, and Glamis Castle is one of the most ancient family seats in Great Britain. It was the scene of the murder of Duncan by Macbeth, and its thick walls hold many grim secrets—the most curious one of all being the secret room which is visited when each heir comes of age. Where this secret chamber is, or what it contains,

Balmoral Castle

only three men know—the Earl, his heir, and the factor—and through successive generations that trio has kept the secret inviolate.

The ancient family was founded in Scotland by a member of the de Leonne family of France, who came to England with William the Conqueror. His son, Roger de Leonne, accompanied King Edgar, son of Malcolm Canmore, to Scotland about 1091, and for his services against Donald Bane he was rewarded with lands in Perthshire, which may have given rise to the name Glen-Lyon.

Queen Elizabeth's Ancestors

From this Roger de Leonne was lineally descended Sir John Lyon, whose name was prominent in the reigns of Robert the First and his son David II. Sir Roger got a charter, about 1342, to the lands of Forteviot and Forgandenny in Perthshire. He also had—from David II—a charter of the thanedom of Tannadyce, in Forfarshire, and the reversion of the thanedom of Glamis, in the same county.

The son of Sir John Lyon, who bore the same name as his father, linked the family with royalty. This second Sir John Lyon appears to have been a man of more than ordinary ability, and he became the Secretary to King Robert II. From his royal master he got a charter of the whole lands and thanedom of Glamis, dated March 13th, 1372, and four years later he married Princess Jean Stewart, the second daughter of the King. This brought in the barony of Kinghorn in Fife, and permitted him to wear a lion rampant in his armorial bearings.

Nothing was too good for this son-in-law and favourite of the King. In 1378 he was appointed great-Chamberlain of Scotland, and between 1380 and 1382, he got no less than eight different charters under the Great Seal, which gave him estates all over the north of Scotland. He was killed in a duel in 1383, by a nephew of the king.

His son, John Glamis of Forteviot, became the heir in 1396, and he and his son Patrick became hostages for James I, when that king was released from prison in England. The son Patrick succeeded his father about 1427, taking the title of Lord Glamis, and he became a member of the Privy Council of James II.

The Lyons, in fact, succeeded each other as Privy Councillors for generations, for John, the third Lord Glamis, was a Privy Councillor to James IV. This baron had three sons killed at Flodden, so the family was giving, as well as taking.

Our Queen's Ancestors

And so the record of the Lyons reads, down through the centuries. The 8th Lord Glamis, John, agreed to support the odious marriage of the Earl of Bothwell with Mary Queen of Scots, and during the early years of the reign of Mary's son, James the Sixth, the men of Glamis were active in Court circles. Lord Glamis and Lord Herries were deputed by the nobles in 1577 to bring about the resignation of the Regent Morton—and they induced that sinister despot to resign. This Glamis was slain in a street brawl at Stirling on March 17th, 1598.

The 9th Lord, better known as The Master of Glamis, was mixed up in the kidnapping of King James the Sixth which was known as The Ruthven Raid, and he it was who "layed his leg before the King" when the boy tried to get away. For that act Glamis had to flee to Ireland in 1583, but he returned to Scotland when the wind shifted and was one of the nobles who took part in King James's fantastic "Goodwill banquet" in High Street, Edinburgh, on February 9th, 1586. This was the man who became one of James's Privy Councillors and who served as a Scots Commissioner to treat of a Union with the English Commissioners in 1604.

His eldest son, John, the 2nd Earl of Kinghorn, also became a Privy Councillor, in 1641, and his son obtained a charter, dated July 1, 1677, providing that he "and his heirs male, or heirs whatsoever, should in all future ages be styled earls of Strathmore and Kinghorn, Viscounts Lyon, and Barons Glamis, Tannadyce, Sidlaw and Strathdictie."

Thus did the name Strathmore enter Scottish history. It is one of the most ancient in the country, and connotes, as few names do, a long line of famous men who were high in the councils of State, and bound by the ties of blood to the first king of the House of Stewart.

Queen Elizabeth

Queen Elizabeth, therefore, has royal blood in her veins, and by her marriage to the present King she re-unites the blood of the first Stewart King with the Stewart blood that came back to our Royal Family by way of that other Queen Elizabeth, who, by her marriage with the Count Palatine, brought into existence the Hanoverian Line on which the Succession was established by Act of Parliament.

It is a curious and interesting story, and let us hope that it may be a good omen for the future of our monarchy. Truly, the name Elizabeth has loomed large in British history, and it reappears, strangely enough, in the little Princess who is now heir-presumptive to the throne.

KING GEORGE VI—
of Scotland